SECRET
CAPE COD
AND THE ISLANDS

A Guide to the Weird, Wonderful, and Obscure

Linda Humphrey
and Maria Lenhart

REEDY PRESS

Reedy Press
PO Box 5131
St. Louis, MO 63139
www.reedypress.com

Library of Congress Control Number: 2023951949
ISBN: 9781681065274

Design by Jill Halpin

Unless otherwise indicated, all photos are courtesy of the author or in the public domain.

We (the publisher and the author) have done our best to provide the most accurate information available when this book was completed. However, we make no warranty, guarantee, or promise about the accuracy, completeness, or currency of the information provided, and we expressly disclaim all warranties, express or implied. Please note that attractions, company names, addresses, websites, and phone numbers are subject to change or closure, and this is outside of our control. We are not responsible for any loss, damage, injury, or inconvenience that may occur due to the use of this book. When exploring new destinations, please do your homework before you go. You are responsible for your own safety and health when using this book.

Printed in the United States of America
24 25 26 27 28   5 4 3 2 1

For James Humphrey, the third member
of our Hard News Travel Team

Bass Hole Boardwalk.
Photo by Linda Humphrey

CONTENTS

Provincetown Flag House.
Photo courtesy of Cape Cod
Chamber of Commerce

ACKNOWLEDGMENTS

First, we'd like to thank William P. DeSousa-Mauk, president of DeMa Public Relations, who tirelessly answered our endless requests.

Thank you to everyone who took the time to help us: Richard Archer, Derek Bartlett, Shantaw Bloise-Murphy, Rita Carr, Mary Childs, Charlie Clark, Rob Costa, Meg Costello, Jeremy Davis, Bryce Elizabeth, Brent Ellis, Judith Goetz, Kevin Greenberg, Brien Hefler, Lucy Helfrich, Gregory Hischak, Kim Holl, Tina Holl, Kaylene Jablecki, Bill Jamieson, Pat Jette, Meredith Katz, Pattie Laubhan, Tom Lyons, Malcolm MacNab, Kevin Nadeau, Troy Neuenburg, Mark A. Pearson, Max Pinson, Michael Quinlin, Betsy Rich, Ann Ring, Brent Thomas, John Tiernan, Jennifer Walker, Christopher Wilson, and Taryn Withers.

Thank you to the CLOC actors Laura Lydia Paruzynski, Mitchell McVeigh, Andrey Vdovenko, Rachel Querreveld, Ryan Wolpert and Gabby Gonzalez.

To Jack Humphrey, James Humphrey, Isabel Humphrey, Sheri Humphrey, Allison Simmons, Kristi Towey, Tim Alosi, Marilee Crocker, Amy Miller, and Jo-Ann Miller, who explored the Cape and islands with us, thank you.

To our amazing team at Reedy Press, especially Josh Stevens, Amanda Doyle, Jill Eccher, and Barbara Northcott, thank you.

Finally, we'd like to thank Dr. Rufus Peebles and Blakeney Adlam, who rescued us when we found ourselves stranded on Martha's Vineyard at the remote Orange Peel Bakery with no car or cell phone service to call for a lift. The bakery shack had no attendant; it operates on the honor system, a charming if (in this case) inconvenient aspect of the Vineyard's bucolic up-island towns. It started to rain. In a panic, we asked the first people who stopped by the bakery for a ride into town. That's how we met the charming Dr. Peebles, a vice president of the Harvard Club of Cape Cod (class of '61) and a practicing psychologist, and his great-nephew Blakeney. Sometimes the best travel experiences are those you don't expect.

Moshup Beach.
Photo courtesy of Massachusetts
Office of Travel & Tourism

INTRODUCTION

The theme of this book is appropriate for Cape Cod and the islands, places where the attractions and backstories are subtle and often hidden from view. There's nothing like the Grand Canyon or Niagara Falls here. The scenery is tamer but no less arresting with its luminous skies, broad beaches, bayberry-covered dunes, glacial ponds, salt marshes, cranberry bogs, and stunted forests growing from sandy soil.

Its secrets are many, and they stretch back even before the *Mayflower* landed in what is now Provincetown (it got to Plymouth Rock later). What, for example, is the story behind the Bourne Stone—were its mysterious carvings made by Vikings or early native peoples? Can the so-called witch Goody Hallett still be heard wailing in rage over the dunes at night? Do ghosts really lurk in the stacks of Isaiah Thomas Books or in the chambers of Highfield Hall and the Old Yarmouth Inn?

It's also a place that inspired many of the greatest American authors, playwrights, and painters to form creative communities and produce seminal works. It's where Kurt Vonnegut Jr. blossomed as a novelist, Edward Gorey drew wonderfully gruesome illustrations, Edward Hopper painted landscapes, and Tennessee Williams and Eugene O'Neill found their footing as dramatists. It's also long been the stomping grounds for Hollywood A-listers and the Washington power elite, a varied lot that includes Fred Rogers, Carly Simon, Spike Lee, James Cagney, Grover Cleveland, and assorted Kennedys, Clintons, and Obamas.

We hope this book will inspire you to dig deeper into this multilayered region where the weird, wonderful, and obscure lie just beneath the surface of a deceptively bucolic facade.

SHARK!

What legacy did the filming of *Jaws* leave behind on Martha's Vineyard?

It's been about 50 years since the iconic movie *Jaws* first scared people out of the water, but its filming is still an object of fascination on Martha's Vineyard and Cape Cod. It's easy to catch a screening at Cape movie houses during the summer, whether at the historic Chatham Orpheum Theater or the Wellfleet Drive-In. On Martha's Vineyard visitors can take a self-guided or organized tour of the movie locations, sometimes led by people who were extras on the film set.

But the movie that left an impact on Martha's Vineyard almost wasn't filmed there. In the novel by Peter Benchley, *Jaws* took place on Amity Island, a fictional summer resort off Long Island. Benchley, who had summered on Nantucket during his youth, wanted the movie set there, but the location scout was unable to reach the island because of a storm. Director Steven Spielberg favored Montauk, but the waters off the Long Island town were too deep for the mechanical shark to function. Martha's Vineyard offered much shallower waters, and Edgartown, far less gentrified than it is today, projected a lower-middle-class vibe Spielberg felt was appropriate for a story of villagers worried about their tourism livelihood.

As the first major motion picture to be filmed on Martha's Vineyard, *Jaws* caused quite a stir. Islanders were paid $64 as extras, primarily tasked with running across the beach and screaming. Since the beachgoing extras weren't told the movie was about a shark, Chief Brody's announcement about a shark in the water caused

---

SCARY MOVIE

WHAT: *Jaws* locations

WHERE: Martha's Vineyard, primarily in or near Edgartown

COST: Free

PRO TIP: Edgartown Tours (edgartowntours.com) and Martha's Vineyard Tours and Transport (mvtoursandtransport.com) offer guided *Jaws* tours at various times during the year.

---

a panic that was completely genuine. The movie that was supposed to take 55 days to film ended up taking 159 days due to the significant challenges of filming shark scenes in an actual ocean rather than the usual water tank in Hollywood. When it finally wrapped, the initially welcoming islanders were reportedly glad to see the film crews go home.

Many of the sites from the movie are still around to explore. Among them is the American Legion Memorial or "Jaws" Bridge, which connects Edgartown to Oak Bluffs and is where the shark swims underneath to ravage a man boating in the placid waters of Sengekontacket Pond. The still-operating Chappy Ferry, which connects Edgartown to Chappaquiddick Island, is where Mayor Vaughn tries to convince Brody that the beaches are safe and should not be closed. Joseph Sylvia State Beach north of Edgartown is where the terrified beachgoers flee from the waters when the Kintner boy is attacked. In the fishing town of Menemsha, the Menemsha Galley restaurant is a good place to view the spot where the *Orca* took off on the final quest to bring the predator to its doom.

Jaws author Peter Benchley later expressed regret over portraying sharks as killing machines and became an advocate for their protection.

Jaws is still a featured attraction at local movie venues like the Wellfleet Drive-In. Photo by James Humphrey

WHERE I LIKE BEING ME

Which *SNL* legend is buried near his former Martha's Vineyard retreat?

His gravesite drew so many visitors that it had to be moved. Fans had trampled the ancient Martha's Vineyard cemetery, leaving sunglasses, beer bottles, beach stones, and cigarettes. His new headstone, which some have compared to a Halloween decoration, includes the epitaph "I May Be Gone, but Rock and Roll Lives On."

John Belushi—of *Saturday Night Live*, *Animal House*, and *The Blues Brothers* fame—and his wife, Judy, bought a Vineyard beach house from Robert McNamara in 1979. The couple—high-school sweethearts from the Chicago area—spent just a few summers on the island, where Belushi said "this is where I like being me," along with neighbors Dan Aykroyd and Bill Murray. In 1982, the 33-year-old actor died from a drug overdose in Hollywood.

He had once said he'd like a Viking funeral, but his mother objected, and he was buried in Chilmark's Abel's Hill Cemetery. A year later, his gravesite was moved to a section near the road. (This proved to be messy, as the coffin broke and a new one had to be flown in from Boston.) Surrounded by a rustic split-rail fence, a large beach rock is inscribed with "Belushi," and then, a few feet away, there's the 17th century–style tombstone, engraved with a skull and crossbones.

To mark the one-year anniversary of Belushi's death, family and friends gathered at the Aquinnah Cliffs for a Viking funeral of sorts.

Wondering why 17th-century headstones were so creepy, with skulls, crossbones, hourglasses, and the like? These motifs are *memento mori*, reminders of mortality and a warning to live a virtuous life.

Rumors persist that Belushi is actually buried in an unmarked grave. Inset: *On the Vineyard, John and Judy could be found at Lucy Vincent Beach. Photo by Jeremy Zolkowski*

GRAVE SIGHT

WHAT: Where wild *SNL* comic and movie star John Belushi is buried

WHERE: Abel's Hill Cemetery, Chilmark

COST: Free

PRO TIP: "Just like everyone else, we fell in love with Lucy Vincent Beach," Judy had said. Visit this private Chilmark beach by staying at a nearby inn or rental house, or arrive after mid-September.

They placed mementos on a small boat, including a scrapbook Judy had made for John's 29th birthday, a pack of cigarettes, a cross, a guitar pick, a microphone, and an unpaid IOU made out to Bill Murray. As the group huddled together on the chilly beach, they watched the ship, set on fire, disappear over the horizon.

SOUND OF SUMMER

Where can you get hugs from up-and-coming young singers?

Like beach days and ice cream, this group of 10 college guys in Vineyard Vines outfits is a requisite part of a Cape Cod summer. They draw crowds all over the Cape, from resorts to backyard barbecues.

"We try to exude joy and to bring people happiness throughout the summer," said Max Pinson, member and business manager of Hyannis Sound, the Cape's beloved a cappella group.

Family friendly and a bit nostalgic, Hyannis Sound keeps its shows light and fun, "even as college a capella gets a little edgier," Pinson said, with weekly concerts in Falmouth, Chatham, Hyannis, and Brewster. Between songs like Jackie Wilson's "(Your Love Keeps Lifting Me) Higher and Higher" and the Temptations' "My Girl," the guys add funny stories about their childhoods or escapades on the Cape. These tales change each night, as their many devotees catch multiple shows.

After each concert, they greet fans—hugging, taking selfies, and chatting, sometimes for an hour or more. These impromptu after-parties happen at their private gigs as well, whether they're at the Chatham Bars Inn, a yacht-club wedding, or a kids' birthday party. "It often feels like we are half entertainment but also half guests," Pinson said.

Amid all this camaraderie and upbeat energy, it's easy to forget that Hyannis Sound, which was founded in 1994, is a professional

HYANNIS SOUND A CAPPELLA GROUP

WHAT: 10 college-aged singers from across the country

WHERE: Weekly concerts in Falmouth, Chatham, Dennis, and Hyannis

COST: $15 adults, $10 seniors and children under 10

PRO TIP: Check out the Cape's all-female college a cappella group, Cape Harmony, as well: capeharmony.org.

Before each weekly concert, these 10 guys pop in to sing at local restaurants. Photo courtesy of Hyannis Sound

group that auditions more than 100 singers across the country each year with an acceptance rate of less than 5 percent. Alumni have performed on Broadway and on *America's Got Talent*. Even so, Pinson said, the group "has that ragtag feel that I think people want when you're hiring 10 college guys to sing at your party."

Hyannis Sound alums Max Pinson and Brendan Jacob Smith were cast in the 2023 national tour of *The Simon & Garfunkel Story.*

STAR SANCTUARY, PART ONE

Why is Martha's Vineyard known as Hollywood East?

It may be less pretentious in style than Beverly Hills or the Hamptons, but Martha's Vineyard during the summer draws its share of show business A-listers and other assorted VIPs. So much so that the island is sometimes referred to as Hollywood East.

Tucked deep into the leafy glades or along the dunes of private beaches are the pricey abodes of rock musicians and some of the world's biggest TV and film stars. To name a few, Carly Simon, James Taylor, Meg Ryan, Michael J. Fox, Jake and Maggie Gyllenhaal, Bill Murray, Ted Danson, Mary Steenburgen, Amy Schumer, Spike Lee, and Chelsea Handler are among the local citizenry who call the island home for part of the year.

For visitors hoping to learn more about the Vineyard's famous residents, taking a van tour of the island is one way to do it. We found this to be true on a three-hour tour offered by Oak Bluffs Land and Wharf Co. where our affable guide, Troy Neuenberg, was a fount of information on local celebrities past and present. As we headed out of Oak Bluffs, Troy pointed out a stately waterfront mansion once owned by Gloria Swanson, silver-screen legend and mistress of Joseph Kennedy, patriarch of the Kennedy clan.

Unlike most island celebrities who only summer on Martha's Vineyard, singer-songwriter Carly Simon has owned a year-round residence there, currently a 27-acre compound in Tisbury called Hidden Star Hill, since the 1970s. Also a longtime local property owner, Simon's ex-husband James Taylor bought 175 acres of woodlands on the island with the first proceeds from his recordings.

The Chilmark General Store, where Larry David and Alan Dershowitz had a frosty exchange, is a meeting ground for celebrities and regular folks alike. Right: *Longtime resident Carly Simon has given many benefit concerts on the island.*

He explained that Swanson was not the first Hollywood star to seek out the peace and seclusion of Martha's Vineyard. That is believed to be James Cagney, who purchased a 200-acre farm in Chilmark in 1936. "He lived on the Vineyard for many years and would take groups of local schoolkids, most of whom rarely got off the island, on field trips to Washington, DC, to see the monuments and museums," Troy said.

OAK BLUFFS LAND AND WHARF CO.

WHAT: Company offering van tours of Martha's Vineyard

WHERE: 9 Circuit Ave. Extension, Oak Bluffs

COST: $56.50

PRO TIP: Don't expect to spot local celebrities driving fancy cars. Many keep modest vehicles, known as "island cars," that help them keep a low profile and also withstand the island's dirt roads and rough terrain.

Driving into Chilmark, Troy noted that the rustic Chilmark General Store is one of the places on Martha's Vineyard where celebrities frequently shop, as are the Cronig's and Reliable grocery markets in various island locations. Encountering each other in the Chilmark General Store a few years ago, *Seinfeld* cocreator Larry David and famed attorney Alan Dershowitz got into a political argument so heated that it drew national attention when it made the *New York Post*'s Page Six gossip column.

Up the road a few miles, Troy pointed out an ordinary-looking mailbox belonging to Seth Meyers, who broadcast some of his *Late Night with Seth Meyers* episodes from his island home during the pandemic. According to Troy, he's a good local citizen.

"He supports pop-up food banks and does fundraisers to benefit working people on the island, recognizing how expensive it is for them to live here," he said.

CAMPY SITE

What inspired all those gingerbread cottages in Oak Bluffs?

To make a short right turn off of Circuit Avenue in Oak Bluffs is to suddenly leave the modern world behind and enter a fairy-tale enclave of little sherbet-colored Victorian cottages surrounding a grassy park with an open-sided pavilion in the center. This is the enchanting domain of the Martha's Vineyard Camp Meeting Association, which has its roots in 1835, when a group of local Methodists began holding religious meetings on the site. Families began flocking to the outdoor services, often setting up tents for several days each summer.

By the 1860s, the encampment had grown to over 200 tents, and the families, by now often extending their stays into long summer sojourns, wanted more permanent shelter. Designed to replicate the convivial spirit of the canvas tents, the 500 cottages constructed in the area featured steep pitched roofs, double doors, and front porches conducive for conversation with neighbors and passersby. Thanks to a new-fangled invention, the power-driven jigsaw, carpenters were able to outdo each other with ornate woodwork and a riot of gingerbread trim. In later years, some cottage owners stepped things up by painting their cottages in vibrant color combinations, pairing salmon pink with lime green or powder blue with burgundy red.

TINY HOMES

WHAT: Martha's Vineyard Camp Meeting Association Cottage Museum

WHERE: 1 Trinity Park, Oak Bluffs

COST: $3

PRO TIP: For a magical evening, attend Grand Illumination Night, which is held during the third Wednesday in August. Residents of the gingerbread cottages light up their homes with Japanese lanterns, and there's a program of music with a community sing-along in the Tabernacle.

The architecture of the gingerbread cottages was meant to recall the shape of the original tents on the site. Photo by Maria Lenhart

Despite the festive appearance of the cottages, the community remained religious in nature, with the Camp Meeting Association erecting fences around the enclave to keep drunks and other unruly outsiders at bay. An iron structure called the Tabernacle was erected in the center of the enclave in 1879, a structure still used for church services (representing a variety of faiths) as well as concerts and other events. Of the original 500 cottages, 315 remain and all are privately owned.

For a look inside a cottage as it was in the 19th century, step into the Gingerbread Cottage Museum & Gift Shop, a two-story charmer adorned with period furnishings and photographs of early camp life. Docent Nancy Blank, herself a cottage resident for over 80 years, explains the joys and challenges of cottage ownership. Despite their tiny size, many sell in the million-dollar range and often require costly insulation for year-round use. The purchase prices does not include the land, which is owned by the Martha's Vineyard Camp Meeting Association.

Some of the gingerbread cottages are available for rent by the individual owners, including through rental sites like Airbnb and Vrbo. Rentals are only available during the summer, usually go for $2,000 to $4,500 per week, and are subject to rules set by the Martha's Vineyard Camp Association.

VINEYARD VANES

What's behind the wild assortment of weathervanes on so many Martha's Vineyard rooftops?

Look upward on Martha's Vineyard and before long you're bound to see a rooftop crowned with a weathervane. Not just an ordinary weathervane, mind you, but a metal sculpture of a rabbit in a tower, a trio of bears paddling a canoe, a cavorting whale, or even a scene inspired by Maurice Sendak's *Where the Wild Things Are*. These are among the fanciful works created by Tuck & Holand Metal Sculptors, a local studio that has crafted thousands of distinctive weathervanes over the years, some of them for such celebrated clients as Steven Spielberg, Carly Simon, James Taylor, and Beverly Sills.

It all started in 1974, when metal sculptor Travis Tuck was approached by Spielberg, then filming *Jaws* on the Vineyard, to create a weathervane in the shape of a great white shark for the top of Captain Quint's shack. Tuck was soon on his way to becoming the world's premier weathervane artist, eventually taking on a young apprentice named August Holand in 1998. Tuck taught Holand the art of *repoussé*, the process of heating sheets of copper metal, dousing them with water to make them malleable, and then hammering out shapes from the reverse side.

In addition to customized weathervanes, Tuck & Holand offers a limited edition selection of pieces for purchase that are signed, numbered, and based on designs developed by Travis Tuck. These include the great white shark originally created for the movie *Jaws*.

Tuck & Holand weathervanes add whimsy to rooftops all over Martha's Vineyard.

Holand has been at the helm of the business, which occupies a workshop and gallery space in Vineyard Haven, since Tuck passed away in 2002. Perhaps the Tuck & Holand weathervane most familiar to island visitors is the one depicting a whale that sits atop the bandstand in Ocean Park in Oak Bluffs.

While many Tuck & Holand weathervanes grace the rooftops of Martha's Vineyard, they can be found far and wide for a variety of clients who are willing to pay a starting price of $15,000 and remain on a waitlist for at least two years. Spielberg is among repeat customers, having commissioned a four-foot velociraptor from *Jurassic Park* to adorn his Long Island home. There's also a weathervane depicting a Twin Hellcat fighter plane hovering above the Nantucket airport and a six-by-four-foot elephant decorating the Philadelphia Zoo. Not all of the weathervanes are perched on rooftops, as many owners choose to display these valuable artworks indoors.

TUCK & HOLAND METAL SCULPTORS

WHAT: A studio and gallery known for distinctive weathervanes

WHERE: 275 State Rd., Vineyard Haven

COST: Customized weathervanes start at $15,000 or more.

PRO TIP: Not in the market for a weathervane? Tuck & Holand also produces sundials, signage, logos, and other metal artworks.

ALLEY'S GENERAL STORYBOOK

Where can you soak up a bit of Vineyard history while stocking up on beach supplies?

With their creaking screen doors and penny candy, 19th-century general stores were social hubs where friends would bump into each other and sip coffee on the front porch.

That hasn't changed on Martha's Vineyard, where Alley's General Store, the island's oldest retail business, has been open in the town of West Tisbury since 1858. This being the Vineyard, the neighbors you bump into just might be the Obamas.

About 150 locals still pick up their mail from a wall of vintage mailboxes, a throwback to Alley's 1927 post office. The hunter-green porch swing matches the double doors next to the posters touting the island's latest film festival. Bags of popcorn spill from an antique Cola-Cola ice chest. If your shopping list includes a ukulele, a dog leash, a bicycle bell, a retro alarm clock, Vidalia Onion Fig Sauce, garlic

ALLEY'S GENERAL STORE

WHAT: Enchanting 19th-century general store

WHERE: 1045 State Rd., West Tisbury, Martha's Vineyard

COST: Free to explore

PRO TIP: Don't miss 7a Foods, the farm-to-takeout restaurant next door. Chef-owner Daniel Sauer is an alum of storied NYC restaurants Craft and Hearth. Hoping to bump into the Obamas? Besides Alley's, they've been sighted at the nearby State Road Restaurant.

Vintage general stores to explore on the Cape include Centerville's 1856 Country Store and the 1866 Brewster Store, which was converted from an 1852 church.

Alley's is a must-stop for anyone driving up-island. Photos by Linda Humphrey

bulbs, a West Tisbury T-shirt, and a large octopus plush toy, you'll find all of that at this cheerful emporium.

In the early 1990s, though, Alley's nearly closed after falling into decline. While many country stores get by on liquor sales, West Tisbury is a dry town. Amid concern that historic general stores were dying out, the Vineyard Preservation Trust, which aims to preserve buildings for their original purposes, acquired and renovated Alley's in 1993.

Known as "a place to find everything you need and didn't know you needed," this island landmark is now open 364 days a year. As one visitor wrote on Tripadvisor, "You can't be in there and be in a bad mood. This place is like the contents of one big Christmas stocking."

DOWN BY THE SEA

Where is the sunset a social scene, inspiring applause and marriage proposals?

Take in the beachy vibe, the salt air, and the showstopping sunset as you stroll the Bass Hole Boardwalk in Yarmouth Port. With 360-degree views of Cape Cod Bay, this boardwalk extending over a salt marsh is one of a handful of spots where the nightly sunset ritual is a social event. Each plank is engraved with a message: engagements, proposals, family vacations. If it's summertime and the tide is high, you can jump off into the water at the end of your walk.

On Martha's Vineyard, the adorable fishing village of Menemsha is the place for cheering, à la Key West, as the sun dips into the water—and as couples get engaged. Two tiny seafood shacks, Larsen's Fish Market and Menemsha Fish Market, are as iconic as the sunset here. Arrive early to snag a parking spot and set up a picnic. (There's also a second parking lot with shuttle service.) Pick up lobster rolls, chowder, oysters, and more—and BYOB, as Menemsha is a dry town.

You'll also find sunsets to set your heart racing all along Cape Cod Bay. Provincetown's Herring Cove Beach and the stretch of Orleans beach that includes both Skaket Beach and Rock Harbor Beach all draw cheering crowds. Other bay-side beaches known for sunset festivity

SUNSET SOCIAL SCENE

WHAT: Bass Hole Boardwalk, Menemsha Public Beach, and other beaches known for sunset gatherings

WHERE: Center St., Yarmouth Port. Menemsha Public Beach, Chilmark, Martha's Vineyard

COST: Free

Bass Hole/Gray's Beach charges $20 for parking before 5 p.m.

PRO TIP: Oak Bluffs Land and Wharf Co. offers private sunset tours to Menemsha. Vans, stocked with refreshments, depart from Oak Bluffs an hour before sunset and pick up an hour after sunset. The trip takes about 30 minutes.

Intoxicating sunsets draw cheering crowds to Menemsha Public Beach on Martha's Vineyard. Photo by Randi Baird

include Sandy Neck Beach in Sandwich, Millway Beach (near the Millway Marina, where the Hyannis Whale Watcher Cruises depart) in Barnstable, and Mayflower, Corporation, and Crowes Pasture Beaches in Dennis. Don't forget the bug spray!

When sunset coincides with low tide, head to Brewster to walk the largest tidal pools in North America, the Brewster Flats. Try Paine's Creek Beach and Crosby Landing Beach.

Menemsha Public Beach. Photo by L.A. Brown

STAR SANCTUARY, PART TWO

Why has Martha's Vineyard been a longtime retreat for famous authors, politicians, and broadcasters?

While an increasing number of show-business celebrities are buying homes on Martha's Vineyard, famous people from the literary, media, and political worlds have been summering on the island for many decades. Among the tidbits learned during our Oak Bluffs Land and Wharf Co. van tour is that ABC News icon Diane Sawyer is a longtime Vineyard resident, as is Chris Wallace, who lives in the island retreat once owned by his father, Mike, of *60 Minutes* fame.

Our guide, Troy, explained that Mike Wallace was close pals with two of his summer neighbors, humorist Art Buchwald and best-selling author William Styron. "All three of them suffered from clinical depression, so much so that they referred to themselves as the Blues Brothers," he said.

Presidential couples Bill and Hillary Clinton and Barack and Michelle Obama are among the political superstars drawn to Martha's Vineyard during the summer. The Clintons spent the first of many summer vacations on the Vineyard in 1993, renting a home on Oyster Pond in Edgartown. Their presence inspired Carol McManus, owner of a local coffee shop called Espresso Love to create a special Presidential Muffin baked with cream cheese and berries for the commander-in-chief, who reportedly dropped by on his bike to try it.

More recently, Barack Obama, who purchased a 30-acre estate on Edgartown Great Pond a few years ago, inspired McManus to create a breakfast treat in his honor. It's a Hawaiian-style muffin baked with banana, pineapple, coconut, and macadamia nuts.

According to Troy, a favorite eatery for the Obama family is Nancy's, a casual seafood restaurant in Oak Bluffs. Presidential daughter Sasha landed a summer job at the restaurant in 2016, handling orders at the takeout window.

Near the end of our island tour, we drove by the most famous property on Martha's Vineyard with presidential associations—Red Gate Farm, a 340-acre spread with a mile of private beach acquired by Jacqueline Kennedy Onassis in 1979. Visible from the highway is the gate and a private road beyond it heading through the woods to the sea. The house and 60 acres surrounding it are now owned by Caroline Kennedy Schlossberg, but the rest of the property has been sold to a conservancy and is protected against development.

"It's a win–win situation for Caroline and those of us on the island who want the land preserved," Troy said.

Judy Blume, Henry Louis Gates Jr., and Geraldine Brooks are among the many esteemed authors with summer homes on Martha's Vineyard. The late Pulitzer Prize–winning biographer and historian David McCullough was also a longtime resident.

Jacqueline Kennedy Onassis purchased Red Gate Farm in 1979.

RENAISSANCE WOMAN

What shaped the literary legacy of Dorothy West?

The little gray-and-white cottage in the Highlands neighborhood of Oak Bluffs, a stop on the African American Heritage Trail of Martha's Vineyard, may look insignificant, but the life of its owner was anything but. She was Dorothy West (1907–1998), a novelist and short-story writer who was part of the intellectual circle of writers, musicians, and artists who embodied what was known as the Harlem Renaissance. West penned much of her work in the modest cottage where she had spent childhood summers long before making it her year-round home in 1947.

Born into an affluent Black family, West spent much of her youth in Boston and Harlem, soon showing a talent for writing by winning literary competitions and publishing short stories while still a teenager. One of her early stories, "The Typewriter," made it into Dodd Mead's annual anthology *The Best Short Stories of 1926*, appearing alongside stories by Ernest Hemingway, Ring Lardner, and Robert Sherwood.

After moving permanently to her family's home in Oak Bluffs, West finished her first novel in 1948, *The Living Is Easy*, a satirical look at an affluent Black family's attempt to climb the social ladder in Boston. For many years she also wrote a column in a local paper, the *Vineyard Gazette*.

It wasn't until late in life that West gained her greatest fame. At the age of 88, she published her second novel, *The Wedding*, which she had written back in 1964 but had decided not to publish because of

---

Along with writing, West also dabbled in acting, winning a small part in the London production of *Porgy and Bess* in 1929. In the 1940s and '50s she was a regular participant in plays staged by the Shearer Summer Theater, a troupe of family and friends in Oak Bluffs.

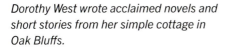

Dorothy West wrote acclaimed novels and short stories from her simple cottage in Oak Bluffs.

DOROTHY WEST HOUSE

WHAT: The residence of a noted Harlem Renaissance novelist

WHERE: Myrtle Ave., Oak Bluffs

COST: No charge to stop by and look at the plaque. The house is not open for tours.

PRO TIP: Not far away is Inkwell Beach, one of the few public beaches on the East Coast where Black people were welcome during the pre–Civil Rights era. The name, originally a racial slur, later became one of pride and a nod to the Harlem Renaissance writers who summered on the island.

the racial climate of the day. With the encouragement of Jacqueline Kennedy Onassis, an island neighbor and editor at Doubleday, she went ahead with publication of the novel, which chronicles the history of a Black family's summers on the Vineyard. The book is dedicated to Mrs. Onassis, who had died shortly before its release in 1995. *The Wedding* soon caught the attention of Oprah Winfrey, whose production company made it into a TV miniseries starring Halle Berry.

With the renewed attention, West became a celebrated figure on the island, and guests at her 90th birthday party included Henry Louis Gates Jr., Jessye Norman, Anita Hill, and Charles Ogletree. Upon her death in 2007, West was noted as the last surviving writer associated with the Harlem Renaissance.

A few years ago the African American Heritage Trail of Martha's Vineyard added her modest home to its landmarks. The plaque on a stone by the house bears West's democratic assertion: "There is no life that does not contribute to history."

TRAIL BLAZERS

Where can you explore African American heritage on Martha's Vineyard?

Thanks to the vision of two friends—Elaine Weintraub, a retired high school teacher, and Carrie Tankard, an active member of the NAACP—a remarkable historical journey unfolds along the ever-expanding African American Heritage Trail of Martha's Vineyard. It started back in 1998 when the women, both concerned over what they viewed as a lack of inclusive history taught in schools, implemented a modest plan to erect four bronze plaques commemorating the extensive but largely untold story of African American history on the island.

Today the Heritage Trail consists of 36 stops with explanatory plaques dotted across Martha's Vineyard, which not only has a long history as a welcoming summer resort for African Americans, but has played a part in everything from the Underground Railroad on up through the Harlem Renaissance and civil rights eras. Along with researching and dedicating landmarks, staff and volunteers at the Heritage Trail organize tours, workshops, and other programs.

Gracing one of the original sites on the trail is a bronze sculpture at Memorial Wharf in Edgartown dedicated to Nancy Michael. Born enslaved, Nancy Michael was believed by seamen in the Edgartown whaling community to be a witch with the power to bless or curse a voyage. Her influence is noted by an 1857 obituary in the *Vineyard Gazette*, which calls her "a most singular character" and asks "may

FOOTSTEPS OF FREEDOM

WHAT: African American Heritage Trail of Martha's Vineyard

WHERE: 36 sites across the island. Detailed information is available at mvaafrican americanheritagetrail.org

COST: Free, if self-guided

PRO TIP: Narrated walking and driving tours of sites along the trail can be booked during the summer.

Plaques across the island are devoted to the African Americans who helped shape the history of Martha's Vineyard.

her good deed live long in our remembrance and her evil be interred with her bones."

Also on Memorial Wharf, a plaque commemorates Esther, a runaway slave who escaped her captor in the dead of night from a ship docked in Edgartown. Another plaque is at the stately Federated Church in Edgartown, where the famed orator and former slave Frederick Douglass spoke in 1857. His visit is observed annually at the church every Independence Day with a reading from a speech in which Douglass posed the question, "What to the slave is the Fourth of July?"

The Overton House, an ornate Victorian facing the waterfront in Oak Bluffs, is another stop. It's a summer retreat once owned by Harlem union organizer Joe Overton, who hosted many prominent African Americans, including Dr. Martin Luther King Jr., Joe Louis, and Jackie Robinson. Nearby on Rose Avenue, Shearer Cottage, believed to be the first African American–owned guesthouse on Martha's Vineyard, welcomed such guests as Paul Robeson, Adam Clayton Powell Jr., and Ethel Waters. It's still owned by a Shearer descendant.

The African American Heritage Trail of Martha's Vineyard is continually expanding. At press time, plans were in the works for a Black Business Trail to include historical examples of Black enterprise and contemporary Black-owned businesses in Oak Bluffs and Vineyard Haven.

CANAL ZONE

What led to Cape Cod's long-awaited engineering marvel?

Its complicated completion solved a problem that had been vexing mariners since Pilgrim times: how to build a canal connecting Buzzards Bay with Cape Cod Bay that would enable ships to bypass the treacherous waters of the outer shores of Cape Cod, the scene of numerous shipwrecks each year. The Cape Cod Canal, often the first thing motorists see as they cross the Bourne or Sagamore Bridge to enter the Cape, is not only used by an estimated 20,000 vessels each year, but is a popular place for visitors to recreate and explore.

A great way to learn about the canal's fascinating but tortuous story is in Sandwich at the waterfront Cape Cod Canal Visitor Center, where interactive exhibits include virtual boat rides and monitors scanning transiting vessels. A video explains that while proposals existed for three centuries, no action took place until a wealthy financier named August Belmont backed and organized construction of the canal that started in June 1909. After his crew surmounted delays caused by bad weather and massive boulders, the waterway opened on July 29, 1914, just ahead of another ambitious project—the Panama Canal. However, Belmont's canal proved a financial failure as mariners were discouraged by tricky currents, narrow bridge openings, high tolls, and other obstacles.

Finally, in 1928 the US government took over ownership of the canal and assigned the US Army Corps of Engineers to undertake its reconstruction, a herculean effort that extended through the

---

The US Army Corps of Engineers is still responsible for maintaining the canal as well as the 1,100 acres surrounding the waterway, which offer picnic areas, campgrounds, hiking trails, and a path along the canal for walking, cycling, and in-line skating.

A highlight of a Cape Cod Canal cruise is the Buzzards Bay Railroad Bridge. Photo by Paul Scharff

HY-LINE CRUISES

WHAT: Company offering scheduled cruises on the Cape Cod Canal

WHERE: 184 Onset Ave., Onset

COST: $21–$23 adults, $12–$13 children

PRO TIP: Hy-Line offers themed cruises during the summer, including those featuring sunset cocktails, musical bingo, and live music.

1930s, providing much-needed employment during the Great Depression. By 1940, the canal was finally a viable operation, a 17.4-mile-long waterway that saves ships from traveling the extra 172 miles to get around the Cape.

As a way to truly experience the canal, Hy-Line Cruises offers a variety of two- and three-hour excursions from the town pier in Onset, a charming hamlet of Victorian-era cottages and tiny harbor islands. Heading past weather-beaten piers, some topped with osprey nests, a canal cruise is a leisurely journey marked by waterfront mansions, the Massachusetts Maritime Academy, Aptucxet Trading Post, and three bridges, including the remarkable Buzzards Bay Railroad Bridge that rises up to accommodate vessels and trains.

PILGRIMS' CONVENIENCE STORE

Where did Plymouth Colony settlers go when they ran out of sugar and clay pipes?

While there is controversy over whether it stands on the original site, the Aptucxet Trading Post and Museum provides a fascinating look at the roots of commerce in America. Built by the Bourne Historical Society in 1930, it's a replica of the original post established in 1627 by pilgrims from the Plymouth Colony as a way to exchange goods with the Wampanoag Indians and Dutch traders from New Amsterdam, now New York.

In the right spot or not, the structure, which is built from 17th-century materials from a house in Rochester, Massachusetts, looks right at home in the grassy 12-acre site overlooking the Cape Cod Canal, once the Manamet River. After stepping over the high threshold for a tour, we were greeted by docent Jeremy Davis, who told us the wide floorboards beneath our feet were fine examples of "king's boards" that were milled from virgin forests to be shipped to England.

"It was a serious offense for colonists to use the king's boards for their own homes, but some did," he said. "If you were caught, you could be hanged."

The beautifully crafted two-room replica features hand-hewn beams, goat-hair plaster, a large brick fireplace with iron cooking implements and, to one side, a primitive still for making beer. There

APTUCXET TRADING POST AND MUSEUM

WHAT: Replica of a Pilgrim-era trading post

WHERE: 6 Aptucxet Rd., Bourne

COST: $6 adults, $4 children

PRO TIP: Pack a picnic lunch. The lovely grounds offer picnic tables, walking trails, and stellar views of the Cape Cod Canal.

Although a replica, Aptucxet was built with materials dating from the 17th century.
Photos by Linda Humphrey

are cases filled with artifacts excavated at the site, including Dutch pottery shards, clay pipes, deer-bone tools, arrowheads, and fishing gear. The museum's most curious artifact is the Bourne Stone, a 300-pound chunk of granite with two lines of ancient carving that has puzzled archaeologists for years. Once thought to have Norse origins, it's now believed to be the work of Native Americans in the area.

Also on display are wampum, purple quahog clamshells fashioned into beads that were vital currency back in the day. Wampum, along with furs, tobacco, sugar, and other household staples, were among the goods frequently exchanged at the post.

Aptucxet, the first of several trading posts established by early New England colonists, did not last long. "It was severely damaged by a hurricane in 1635, one of the worst ever on record," Davis said.

The museum, which works with a liaison from the Wampanoag tribe, hosts informative programs for school groups and special events. Along with enjoying the museum, visitors can also explore the grounds, which include a colonial-style herb garden, a replica of an 18th-century saltworks, a Dutch-style windmill, and the charming Gray Gables train station, which served President Grover Cleveland during his summer holidays.

On the grounds near the museum, the Joseph Jefferson Windmill was originally an art studio for Joseph Jefferson, a celebrated actor at the turn of the 20th century. The structure, a replica of a classic Dutch windmill, was moved from Jefferson's farm in 1976 and has been used as a studio by local artists.

WHITE HOUSE TO GRAY GABLES

Which US President had a private train station on the Cape?

Long before the Kennedys, another US president set up a Summer White House on Cape Cod. He is the only president, so far, to have served two nonconsecutive terms and the only one, so far, to have gotten married in the White House. His 21-year-old bride, Frances—27 years his junior—is the youngest First Lady in history.

He started the tradition of Christmas-tree lights after stringing them around the First Family's tree in 1895. And he traveled to Washington from a private train station, which is now a mini museum in Bourne. Meet Grover Cleveland, the 22nd and 24th president of the United States, a New York Democrat elected in 1885 and 1893.

This sweet 19th-century train station was built for the First Family.
Photo by Linda Humphrey

After losing the 1888 election (but winning the popular vote), Cleveland was drawn to Bourne by his friend and fellow fishing enthusiast Joe Jefferson, a famous actor known for playing Rip Van Winkle. The Clevelands scooped up a summer estate on Buzzards Bay—with "a cheery neighbor in Joe Jefferson at his home among the pines," the *New York Times* reported—which they called Gray Gables.

After winning the presidency again, Cleveland and his family continued to decamp to Gray Gables each summer, launching the tradition of the Summer White House. To skip the horse-drawn carriage ride from the Buzzards Bay station, the railroad line was extended to a private depot near the Cleveland mansion.

Now part of an open-air historical museum, the cottage-like railway station showcases all things Grover Cleveland. (Did you know that his daughter Ruth, known as Baby Ruth in the press, inspired the candy bar's name?) While the Cleveland estate burned down in 1973, their neighborhood is now known as Gray Gables.

GRAY GABLES RAILROAD STATION

WHAT: 19th-century station built for President Grover Cleveland during his second term, now a mini museum.

WHERE: 6 Aptucxet Rd., Bourne

COST: $6

PRO TIP: The Lobster Trap, a classic seafood shack with a patio on the Back River, draws a crowd. It's worth the wait.

October brings a parade of lantern-carrying witches to the Gray Gables neighborhood. A charity walk, the adult-only event features scores of women in witch costumes, with brew stations along the route offering drinks and a chance to mingle with neighbors.

HEART OF GLASS

How did Sandwich become a mecca for fine glassware?

While sand is used to make glass, the fact that Sandwich is close to sandy beaches is not why Deming Jarves chose the town for the site of his Boston & Sandwich Glass Co. back in 1825. He knew that beach sand is too impure to make glass. What attracted Jarves was the town's timber supply, its harbor, and speculation that a canal would be built to make shipping easier (it happened, but not until the Cape Cod Canal opened in 1914).

With the help of master glassblowers, many from England and Ireland, Jarves became known worldwide for blown and mold-blown glassware. In the 1840s and '50s, his company perfected the technique of making pressed glass, a process that eliminated surface impurities. The results were lamps, tableware, candlesticks, vases, perfume bottles, and other items in a dazzling array of shapes and colors. Other glass manufacturers also set up shop in Sandwich during the 19th century, but the Jarves factory closed down in 1888, and by the 1920s the local glass industry had died out due to strikes and other economic factors.

Today, however, Sandwich's glass heritage is stewarded by the Glass Town Cultural District, an entity promoting visitor attractions like the outstanding Sandwich Glass Museum and studio/galleries like Cape Cod Art Glass by Michael Magyar. The district selected Magyar to create the *Glass Obelisk*, a seven-foot-tall public art piece lit from within and fashioned with shards of glass from the old

SANDWICH GLASS MUSEUM

WHAT: Museum devoted to the history of glassmaking in Sandwich

WHERE: 129 Main St., Sandwich

COST: $12 adults, $2 children

PRO TIP: Looking for a good sandwich in Sandwich? Try Café Chew at 4 Merchants Rd. For dessert, head to nearby Ice Cream Sandwich to enjoy ice cream spread between cookies or donuts.

factory site as well as from contemporary artists. It adorns the lawn next to the Dexter Grist Mill at the edge of Shawme Pond.

The Sandwich Glass Museum tells the story of the Boston & Sandwich Glass Co. through chronological exhibits of the exquisite wares produced there. There are also frequent glassblowing demonstrations, special exhibits of contemporary glass art, and a shop selling reproductions.

Not only known for glass, Sandwich is the site of First Church, sometimes called the Elvis Church. That's because Elvis chose a photo of the stately edifice to grace the cover of his *How Great Thou Art* gospel album released in 1967.

The Sandwich Glass Museum illustrates the story of local glassmaking through colorful exhibits and glassblowing demonstrations. Photos by Maria Lenhart

CROWDED HOUSE

What home has stayed off the real estate market since 1641?

For anyone who wants a realistic look at how generations of a Cape Cod family lived from the very early days of colonial settlement up until the 1940s, there's no better place for this than the Wing Fort House, which has sat surrounded by bucolic fields in East Sandwich since 1641. Built by a family of Quakers named Wing, it's distinguished not because of its architecture or the fame of its inhabitants, but by the fact that it's the oldest house in New England continually owned by the same family. Although no Wing has lived there since 1942, the house, which is open to the public from mid-June until mid-September, is owned and maintained by the Wing Family of America, an organization representing as many as 60,000 descendants worldwide.

While the simple white farmhouse was expanded and updated architecturally in the 18th century, later innovations such as electricity and indoor toilets were never considered necessary, according to David Wheelock, a historical archaeologist who greets visitors and shows them around.

With as many as 14 people crammed into the handful of tiny upstairs sleeping rooms, the modern notions of privacy and creature comforts did not exist, he said. "People did not spend much time in the house—it was just for eating and sleeping. Most of the time they were out working in the fields."

Among the most poignant items in the house are the handful of toys scattered among the bedchambers, items that Wheelock explained were not often in use as children worked hard from a

The oldest part of the house is known as "the Fort" because it was built to ward off possible attacks by Native Americans. None ever happened.

The Wing Fort House is the oldest house continually inhabited by one family in New England. Photos by Maria Lenhart

WING FORT HOUSE

WHAT: The oldest house in New England owned by one family

WHERE: 63 Spring Hill Rd., East Sandwich

COST: $5

PRO TIP: Just across the street from the Wing Fort House is the Wing Memorial History Center, a research center with rotating historical exhibits.

young age. Among the household children were indentured servants, some of them as young as 5, who had been contracted into years of servitude by their parents.

Much of the house is furnished with original Wing family antiques as well as some of the more than 10,000 artifacts, among them arrowheads, clay pipes, and crockery, that archaeologists have unearthed around the property. Glass panels cut into the floors reveal some of these findings. Especially well preserved is the "best parlor" with its bannister-back chairs and elegant Georgian-style fireplace, which Wheelock noted was only used on the rare occasions when important visitors came to call. A small heart carved into the parlor's "courting door" enabled the adults to discreetly watch over a young couple in the midst of courtship.

No privacy, indeed.

SWEET SPOT BY SMILING POOL

Where can you explore Peter Rabbit's garden and make your own jam?

Pots of berries, plums, and sugar have been bubbling away since 1903 in the kitchen of an old shingled house set in a wooded landscape that inspired conservationist and author Thornton Burgess to create Peter Rabbit, Jimmy Skunk, Grandfather Frog, Reddy Fox, and other denizens of the Old Briar Patch and Smiling Pool. Today his legacy—and that of his good friend Ida Putnam—lives on at the Thornton Burgess Green Briar Nature Center & Jam Kitchen.

Inside the little house in East Sandwich maintained by the Thornton Burgess Society is a small library and museum of memorabilia devoted to the author, who grew up nearby and penned *Old Mother West Wind* in 1910. Ida Putnam, who owned the house, created the spacious kitchen with its massive 23-burner stove, where she concocted delicious jams and jellies known all over the Cape. Burgess heartily approved of her endeavors, writing to her in 1939 that "'tis a wonderful thing to sweeten the world which is in a jam and needs preserving."

The jam-making tradition is carried on by Emalee Pierce, who offers classes for small groups of individuals and families using the original stove. The former caterer with a degree in aquatic biology makes the many jam varieties, including some from the wild beach

JAMMIN' TIME

WHAT: Thornton Burgess Green Briar Nature Center & Jam Kitchen

WHERE: 6 Discovery Hill Rd., East Sandwich

COST: Free ($5 suggested donation)

PRO TIP: Take time to walk through the nature center's Shirley G. Cross Wildflower Garden, a living museum devoted to the study and use of wildflowers, with over 300 species.

Above: *Emalee Pierce.* Inset: *A delightful place where jam-making and a children's book favorite come together. Photos by Maria Lenhart*

plums abundant in the area, for sale in the gift shop. Like Ida, she keeps things simple and natural.

"The jams are made the old-fashioned way from just fruit and sugar—no pectin, maybe just a little lemon juice or crystalized ginger," Pierce said. "The classes are a fun thing to do, with my goal to keep everyone relaxed and comfortable. You get to leave with five or six jars of your own jam."

The gardens and grounds, which are frequently used for children's nature activity programs, are living illustrations of Thornton Burgess's world of woodlands and native creatures. Trails through the Green Meadow Forest evoke places from his stories, including the Old Briar Patch and Smiling Pool. Look carefully and you just might spy Jerry Muskrat or Reddy Fox scampering away.

There are actually two Peter Rabbits. Thornton Burgess introduced a Peter Rabbit character in the early 1900s, a few years after Beatrix Potter had already done the same.

ABBEY ROAD

**Where can you sleep under a stained-glass window fit
for a Gothic cathedral?**

When Christopher Wilson, a financial planner from Connecticut, purchased a ramshackle old Victorian-era rectory in Sandwich in 1993, he had no idea it would usher in a new life as innkeeper and restaurateur overseeing a growing assortment of one-of-a-kind properties next to each other on a leafy block of Jarves Street. Wilson got to work transforming the rickety manse, where the priest at the adjacent church once lived, into the Painted Lady, a pink-and-white confection with nine bedrooms that became the first component of the Belfry Inn & Bistro.

A few years later Wilson acquired the brick edifice next door, a deconsecrated Catholic church built in 1901, and named it the Abbey. In a stunning example of adaptive reuse, the Abbey's rich oak paneling and glorious stained-glass windows are found throughout the Bistro restaurant and upstairs guestrooms. The church's former confessional now stores the Bistro's wine and liquor supply, while the bar and guest room headboards were fashioned out of the former pews. Each guest room, many of them appointed with spa tubs and fireplaces, is named for a day of the week, reflecting the six days of creation. The standout is the Tuesday Room, with its magnificent Compass window fanning out behind the bed.

Moving up the street, the Belfry's next expansion came in 2003 with Wilson's acquisition of the Village Inn. The 1824 Federal-style house with a wide veranda had gone through many phases over the years, including serving as a boarding house and offices for the company that built the Cape Cod Canal. It now offers four bedrooms decorated in an understated Cape Cod beach theme with

---

The Belfry Inn & Bistro offers wine tasting, live jazz evenings, holiday menus, and other special events throughout the year.

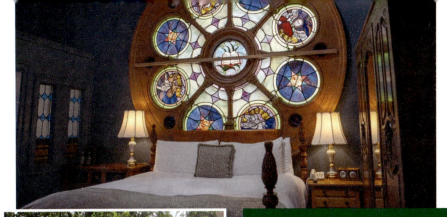

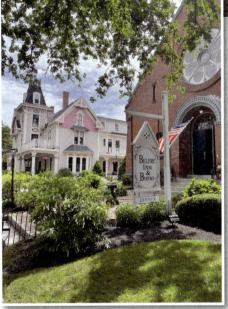

A deconsecrated Catholic church has been transformed into a luxury inn.
Photo by Linda Humphrey

crisp white linens, pastel colors, and wicker furniture. The most recent addition, yet another contrast in style, came in 2021 with the opening of the Seal on the corner of Jarves and Main, an art gallery with a casual bar and eatery converted from a 1931 pharmacy with exposed brick walls and a white tin ceiling overhead.

Is it any wonder that Wilson describes his enterprise as "an architectural tour de force?"

SENTIMENTAL JOURNEY

Where can you pair gourmet dining with a retro train experience?

Sipping prosecco and tucking into fresh cod with lemon-butter sauce and asparagus spears while a passing scene of cranberry bogs, quaint villages, and salt marshes unfolds outside the window . . . it may be the surest way to fall in love with old Cape Cod. It's among the experiences available from the Cape Cod Central Railroad, which operates a variety of train excursions out of Hyannis and Buzzards Bay on vintage railcars powered by the same New Haven FL9 locomotives that once ran on the tracks back in the 1950s and '60s.

The excursions are the last vestiges of the once-extensive local train service that began in 1848 with freight service operated by the Boston & Sandwich Glass Co. This was soon followed by a network of passenger rail lines that once connected nearly all towns on the Cape during the 19th and early 20th centuries. Almost all of this service was discontinued in the late 1950s, and many of the tracks have since been removed, some replaced by the Shining Sea Bikeway and Cape Cod Rail Trail. The Cape Cod Central Railroad, named for an earlier 19th-century rail company, was founded in 1999 as a heritage line and runs on the remaining 27 miles of track from Hyannis to Buzzards Bay.

CAPE COD CENTRAL RAILROAD

WHAT: A heritage railroad line offering train excursions between Hyannis and Buzzards Bay from May through October

WHERE: 252 Main St., Hyannis

COST: $65–$160, depending on excursion and class of service

PRO TIP: Along with the Dinner Train, ride-and-dine experiences include two-hour lunch excursions, brunches with live jazz, and excursions featuring wine or beer tasting from local vintners and brewers.

The Cape Cod Central Railroad dinner excursion includes an elegant meal and a trip across the Cape Cod Canal. Left: courtesy of Massachusetts Office of Travel & Tourism

On a rainy June evening in Hyannis, having booked the three-hour Dinner Train excursion, we boarded a handsome dome car with tables set with white linen to partake of a leisurely five-course dinner that included an appetizer plate of crudités, creamy chowder, salad, dessert, and a choice of entrées with beef, seafood, chicken, and vegetarian options. Jazz standards played on the sound system interspersed with narration on the misty landscape outside, including vast wetlands, dunes, hardwood forests, deep kettle ponds formed by ancient glaciers, and other places not accessible by car.

Before the train headed back for the return journey to Hyannis, we crossed the Cape Cod Canal on the famous Buzzards Bay Railroad Bridge. Lowered to ground level to let our train cross, the bridge can also rise as high as 135 feet when ships need to pass underneath. Not long after we finished our banana cream pie, the train chugged back into Hyannis, and soon we were once again stuck in highway traffic.

In November and December, Cape Cod Railroad operates the Polar Express™ Train Ride, a 90-minute excursion with a visit from Santa along the way. There's also onboard entertainment, gifts for children (who are encouraged to wear their Christmas jammies), hot chocolate, snickerdoodles, and a reading from the classic children's book of the same name.

COFFEE TO GIVE A HOOT ABOUT

How did owl sightings inspire a unique café and roastery?

Soon after entering Snowy Owl Coffee Roasters in Sandwich, it's apparent that this is something other than a typical coffee shop. Dominating the bright, airy expanse is a vibrant mural depicting coffee trees and other elements in the coffee production process. Along with the usual offerings of scones, muffins, and croissants is an assortment of empanadas, the flaky hand pies with savory fillings native to Latin America. These features, along with the name of the place, are clues to an unusual backstory stretching from Peru to Cape Cod.

Manuel Ainzuain and his wife, Shaya Ferullo, found inspiration for Snowy Owl Coffee shortly after the family patriarch, Cesar Ainzuain, died in Peru in 2013. Cesar in his last months had found comfort and amusement from an owl-shaped pillow the family had brought to him in the hospital. After his passing, his children began experiencing numerous owl sightings in disparate locations that included trees in southern Oregon, a parking structure in Miami, the mountains of Peru, and the beaches of Cape Cod.

"The snowy owl is a gift to all Cape Codders; this beautiful animal is an extra-special gift to our family," Manuel said.

Manuel and Shaya, who had recently moved to the Cape from California to be near Shaya's family, established their first Snowy

In many cultures, owls represent wisdom, knowledge, change, transformation, and intuitive development. They're also associated with the spiritual symbolism of death and its relationship to new beginnings and higher understanding.

Snowy Owl is known for Peruvian-style empanadas as well as signature coffee blends.

RAPTOR RAPTURE

WHAT: Snowy Owl Coffee Roasters

WHERE: 161 Rte. 6A, Sandwich; 2624 Main St., Brewster; 483 Main St. (April through December), Chatham

COST: Varies

PRO TIP: Check out Great Cape Herbs, an herb and crystal shop behind Snowy Owl in Brewster.

Owl location in Brewster in 2015. It's a cozy spot with comfy seating, a woodstove, and 200-year-old reclaimed barn wood. It was soon followed by a small café in Chatham. The Snowy Owl in Sandwich came next and now serves as the location for the coffee-roasting operations and the bakery, which turns out the empanadas inspired by Ainzuain's Peruvian homeland.

Committed to using fair-trade beans and improving the lives of local growers, Snowy Owl has direct trade relations with coffee farmers in three regions of Peru. Among its signature blends are Jaws, Captain Crosby, Brewster, and Inka Espresso. Fans of the coffee can join the HOOT Coffee Club, an automatic delivery service that ships whole-bean and ground blends to subscribers.

GEARHEAD GARAGE

What makes the Cape a paradise for fans of classic cars?

Motorists driving along the byways of Cape Cod are often surprised by the number of vintage vehicles they see—perhaps a sweet baby-blue Thunderbird from the 1950s or even a basic black Model T from the 1910s. Somehow they all seem right in sync with the nostalgic atmosphere of the region.

Some of the drivers no doubt belong to one of the vintage car clubs that abound on Cape Cod. The oldest is the Cape Cod Classic Car Club, which started in the 1950s and meets regularly at the Dennis Police Department. The club sponsors numerous car events, including Cruise Nights held on summer Saturdays in Patriot Square in Dennis. It's a showcase for all kinds of vehicles, including classic antiques, muscle cars, trucks, restoMods (restored and modified cars and trucks), and the latest EVs.

The American Automobile Collection, located in a Shaker-style round barn at the Heritage Museums & Gardens in Sandwich, is a great place to view classic cars from horseless carriages on up to the wood-paneled station wagons beloved by the families of mid-century America. A standout in the collection is the 1909 White Steamer purchased for the White House by William Howard Taft, making him the first US president to be transported by car rather than horse and carriage. The steam-powered vehicle enabled Taft to ward off pesky press photographers with bursts of steam.

CAR BARN

WHAT: American Automobile Collection at the Heritage Museums & Gardens

WHERE: 67 Grove St., Sandwich

COST: $22 adults, $12 children

PRO TIP: Heritage Museums & Gardens hosts Gearhead Garage events throughout the year in which car enthusiasts can look under the hoods of the classic vehicles and learn what it takes to maintain them.

The American Automobile Collection pays homage to the family station wagon. Photo by Linda Humphrey

Other favorites in the collection include a 1962 Corvette, built by Chevrolet to rival Ford's Thunderbird, and an early version of a camper-trailer outfitted for a family vacation in the woods. A forerunner of the ubiquitous SUVs of today is the 1946 Mercury Woodie Wagon, a maroon-colored beauty with mahogany paneling and a fold-down tailgate. It came equipped with such modern options as a heater, clock, and radio. Years later, such Woodies were prized by young beachgoers, who found them ideal for transporting surfboards and other gear in places like Cape Cod.

The Toad Hall Classic Sports Car Museum at the Simmons Homestead Inn in Hyannis reflects the passion of innkeeper Bill Putnam for classic English sports cars. His museum exhibits more than 50 sleek and shiny vintage vehicles, most of them British and all of them red. Its name was inspired by Toad, a character in *The Wind in the Willows*, who also loved red motorcars.

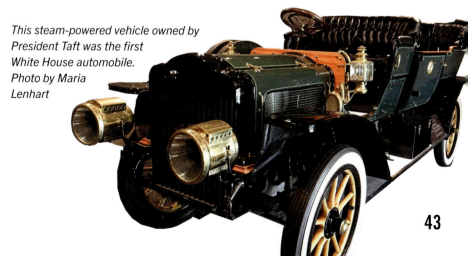

This steam-powered vehicle owned by President Taft was the first White House automobile. Photo by Maria Lenhart

SPIRITS IN THE STACKS

What lurks behind this bookstore's pretty pink facade?

Cape Cod has a wealth of intriguing used bookstores, but none are more so than Isaiah Thomas Books and Prints, with its rabbit warren of rooms piled high with more than 70,000 books on every topic imaginable. The books, running the gamut from well-worn Nancy Drew mysteries to literary classics, first editions, vintage cookbooks, and poetry anthologies, share space with overstuffed couches, stuffed animals, pieces of sculpture, potted orchids, and an assortment of ever-changing oddities. Browsers are apt to encounter a six-foot papier-mâché replica of King Tut's sarcophagus guarding the stacks, a bust of Shakespeare sporting Mickey Mouse ears, or an inflatable orca poised to leap over a bookcase. All of this is contained within an exquisite pink Italianate Victorian house with gingerbread trim, flower boxes, and a turbulent past that belies its gracious exterior.

Owner James Visbeck, who lives upstairs from the store, has stories of the many ghostly encounters and paranormal occurrences he's experienced since buying the place in 1989. Built in the 1860s by the prominent Crocker family, the house transitioned over the years from a residence into a funeral home and has also served as a real estate office, women's clothing store, and summer rental. One day a woman who had once rented the house came into the bookstore and told Visbeck how her friend had fallen down its narrow staircase and broken her knee. The friend insisted the fall was no accident—she felt herself being pushed by an unseen hand.

The bookstore was named in honor of Isaiah Thomas, a revolutionary-era printer and philanthropist who founded the Antiquarian Booksellers of America.

Isaiah Thomas Books and Prints has a charming facade that belies its spooky interior.

Visbeck himself recalls seeing the ghostly, almost transparent image of a woman dressed in a white Victorian dress sitting on the couch in the upstairs apartment. As he passed by the spirit, who resembles one of the Crocker women, she suddenly vanished. While there have been no more sightings, he has seen mysterious depressions in his bed, been awakened by unexplained crashes in the night, and seen the television turn on of its own accord. A further mystery is the large battery-operated clock over the shop counter that, for no apparent reason, often stops at the precise moment Visbeck crosses the threshold whenever he returns from a trip out of town.

Is there a restless spirit roaming the house? Could it be from the long-ago funeral home? Visbeck thinks he may have uncovered a more likely source while renovating the house several years ago. He discovered a tiny secret room hidden under the eaves, completely lined with mattresses. Could this have been a makeshift padded cell confining a troubled member of the Crocker family?

HAUNTED BOOKSTORE

WHAT: Isaiah Thomas Books and Prints

WHERE: 4632 Falmouth Rd., Cotuit

COST: Varies

PRO TIP: Check out the neighboring Cahoon Museum of American Art, which is devoted to fine art and folk art from the 1800s to the present. It features rotating exhibits, artists' talks, and family activities.

PEOPLE OF
THE FIRST LIGHT

Where can you discover Wampanoag history and culture on the Cape?

While English people first came to Cape Cod a little over 400 years ago, the Mashpee Wampanoag Tribe, also known as People of the First Light, are thought to have lived in the region for more than 12,000 years. They are one of two federally recognized tribes of Wampanoag people in Massachusetts—the other is the Wampanoag Tribe of Gay Head on Martha's Vineyard.

With a current population of about 2,800, the Wampanoag once numbered between 30,000 and 100,000 in a land they called Patuxet, which stretched from southeastern Massachusetts to parts of Rhode Island. They made contact with the Pilgrim settlers just months after the *Mayflower* first landed on their shores in 1620, but had actually traded with and sometimes battled Europeans since 1524.

A good place to get an introduction to the tribe's history and culture from the Stone Age to the present is at the Wampanoag Museum in Mashpee. Located in a classic example of an old Cape Cod–style house, the museum rooms are filled with ancient artifacts and heirlooms, among them tools, baskets, hunting and fishing implements, weapons, and kitchen utensils, illustrating the story of the Wampanoag over thousands of years. Especially striking is a large diorama depicting a typical scene from an early Wampanoag settlement.

WAMPANOAG LEGACY

WHAT: Mashpee Wampanoag Indian Museum

WHERE: 414 Main St., Mashpee

COST: $8 adults; $5 children

PRO TIP: Another site to visit is Turtle Wetu, a re-created traditional dwelling and ceremonial venue in Yarmouth Port that serves as an educational center on Wampanoag culture.

Left: *The Mashpee Wampanoag Indian Museum is a Cape-style house filled with ancient treasures. Photo by Maria Lenhart.* Right: *The weety8 is a traditional Wampanoag dwelling. Photo by Linda Humphrey*

The museum grounds feature the Three Sisters Garden, where staples such as squash, beans, and corn are grown; along with a traditional Wampanoag dwelling called a weety8, where the staff demonstrates open-fire cooking and other aspects of daily life. The museum also offers a variety of hands-on activities that include crafting corn-husk dolls and quahog shell shakers.

Not far from the museum is the Old Indian Meeting House, a Greek Revival edifice built in 1758 and the oldest Native American church in the eastern US. A place of great historical and spiritual significance to the Wampanoag, it was the site of the Mashpee Revolt in 1833, when tribal members and their minister protested state intrusions on their self-governance and the theft of their lands by White settlers.

In 1976 the Mashpee Wampanoag Tribe filed a land claim lawsuit, suing the Town of Mashpee for the return of ancestral homelands. They were told by the US District Court that they had no standing to pursue the land claim as they were not a federally recognized tribe. The tribe pursued federal recognition for three decades, finally gaining it in 2007. After more legal struggles, the tribe gained control of 320 acres of land around Cape Cod.

DYLAN'S STRANGEST GIG

What led to Bob Dylan's impromptu concert for a group of middle-aged women playing mah-jongg at a beachfront hotel?

It was November 1975, and famed singer-songwriter Bob Dylan was about to go on the road with a concert tour called the Rolling Thunder Revue. Scheduled to open with two shows in nearby Plymouth, Dylan and an entourage that included singers Roger McGuinn, Joan Baez, Ramblin' Jack Elliott, and poet Allen Ginsberg checked into the Sea Crest Beach Hotel in North Falmouth for a couple of days of rehearsal before the tour began. Being off-season, the only other guests at the secluded hotel on Old Silver Beach were a group of middle-aged housewives participating in a mah-jongg tournament, a kind of Chinese version of dominoes.

The Rolling Thunder Revue, captured in a 2019 documentary of the same title by Martin Scorsese, was intended to be different from most concert tours, featuring an eclectic and changing cast of performers at unusual venues in small cities. The most amusing footage in the documentary captures the moment when Dylan and his cohorts encounter the crowd of women aggressively engaged with their mah-jongg tiles and decide to provide some entertainment. After Ginsberg recites a mournful poetic elegy and Baez sings "Swing Low, Sweet Chariot" in her haunting soprano, Dylan livens things up by banging out a rocking version of his "Simple Twist of Fate" on the piano, sending the ladies into spasms of delight.

SEA CREST BEACH HOTEL

WHAT: Hotel where Bob Dylan rehearsed before a famous concert tour

WHERE: 350 Quaker Rd., North Falmouth

COST: Varies

PRO TIP: Take a short walk from Old Silver Beach to Herring Brook, a salt marsh habitat where you might see egrets, fiddler crabs, and menhaden.

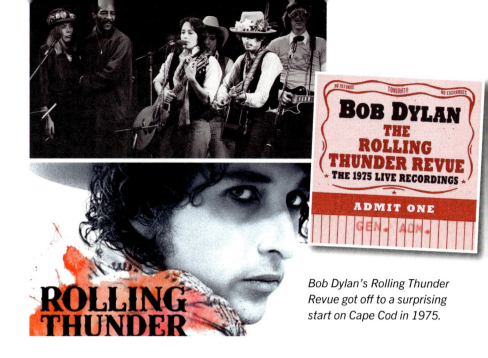

BOB DYLAN
THE
ROLLING
THUNDER REVUE
★ THE 1975 LIVE RECORDINGS ★

ADMIT ONE

GEN · ADM ·

ROLLING
THUNDER

Bob Dylan's Rolling Thunder Revue got off to a surprising start on Cape Cod in 1975.

Dylan also did a lot of rehearsing for the concert while at the Sea Crest. Eight songs that were recorded during the rehearsals at the hotel are included in the *Rolling Thunder Revue* box set of CDs.

While there's little at the hotel today that commemorates Dylan's impromptu appearance, the Sea Crest Beach Hotel still sits on the white sand of Old Silver Beach, its 253 guest rooms decorated in Cape Cod style, some of them with ocean views and fireplaces. It's a popular place to enjoy activities on the private beach, sip a mudslide cocktail on the terrace at sunset, or gather at a holiday buffet in the dining room. Maybe those who listen closely enough can still hear Dylan on the piano with the clink of mah-jongg tiles in the background.

During his stay, Bob Dylan ate at a diner now called Epic Oyster in North Falmouth, a restaurant in a classic Tierney dining car from 1922. A photo of Dylan at the restaurant bar is on the wall at Epic Oyster and can be seen in Martin Scorsese's *Rolling Thunder Revue* documentary on Netflix.

SALTWATER PARK

Where can you ride a natural lazy river?

A chlorine-free lazy river with views of a shimmering bay just might beat a day at the jam-packed water park. Families flock to this "river" at Falmouth's Woodneck Beach, where frolicking kids also scout the tidal pools and marsh for crabs, minnows, shrimp, and more.

Woodneck is rocky, so be sure to add water shoes to your beach-gear list. (There's also plenty of soft white sand.) Pack bodyboards or flotation devices for the river and, if you've got kids, small nets and buckets for scooping up sea creatures.

The lazy river is actually a tidal current that ebbs and flows out from the inlet that connects Little Sippewissett Marsh and Buzzards Bay, said Lucy Helfrich, director of program services for Falmouth's 300 Committee Land Trust. "Because the inlet is constricted and a large volume of water is moving, beachgoers can get a fun ride for 100 yards or so."

The river here isn't quite as lazy as the water-park version, as it doesn't flow in a circle. When the

WOODNECK BEACH

WHAT: Beach with a natural lazy river

WHERE: Woodneck Rd., Falmouth

COST: Free if you get dropped off or go after 5 p.m.

PRO TIP: You'll need a town sticker to park before about 4:30 p.m. If you're staying in Falmouth, you can buy a weekly parking sticker for about $80 at the town beach office.

At low tide, you can walk from Woodneck to hidden Black Beach, a public beach without a parking lot. (Most beachgoers arrive there by boat.)

Grab your donut-shaped pool floats for Woodneck Beach! Photo by Linda Humphrey

tide is going out (from high tide moving toward low tide), you'll ride from the marsh and end up in the bay, and when the tide starts coming in (low tide to high tide), you'll ride the other way, from the bay to the marsh. After a few hours of rides, the river takes a break during slack tide, when the water flow is changing direction.

Google the tides schedule, as this lazy river is controlled by the moon, and to a lesser extent, the sun. What manufactured water park can compete with that?

NEW ENGLAND'S SOUTHERN CHARM

How did a plantation–style mansion end up in a New England historic district?

Colonial- and Federal-style sea captains' homes line Falmouth's Village Green, but Captain Albert Nye's house, with its eight-foot-tall plantation-style pocket windows, transports visitors to the Old South. A wedding gift to the captain's Southern bride in 1849, the Italian Villa–style mansion adds such antebellum features as 13-foot ceilings (rare in the North at the time), a raised foundation, and the pocket windows, which open onto a wraparound veranda.

A New Orleans merchant-ship captain from an old Falmouth family, Nye was hailed as "one of the finest-looking men that ever walked the streets of Falmouth, without any exception," according to town records. His wedding gift was Falmouth's first summer house, complete with a caretaker's cottage across the street at 24 West Main Street (now a private home). Alas, the charming captain was forced to sell the Victorian estate in 1872 after losing his fortune in the Great Panic of 1857.

THE CAPTAIN'S MANOR INN

WHAT: 1849 mansion converted to an inn

WHERE: 27 W Main St., Falmouth

COST: Rates from $165–$410, based on season

PRO TIP: Grab coffee for your village stroll at nearby Coffee Obsession.

Katharine Lee Bates (1859–1929), who wrote the lyrics to "America the Beautiful," grew up across the street, at 16 West Main Street. The Colonial house with a Federal-style doorway, built in 1810, is now a private home.

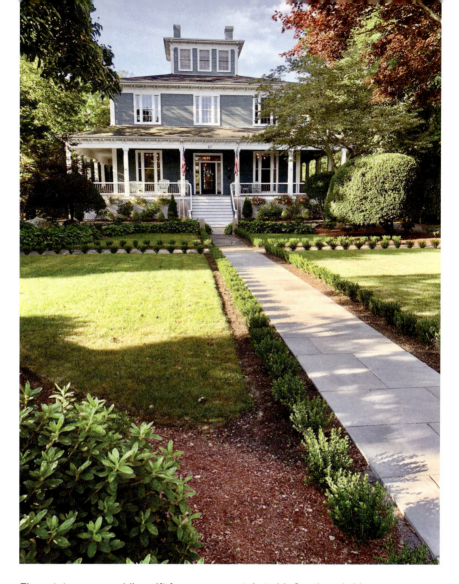

The estate was a wedding gift from a sea captain to his Southern bride.

Now the Captain's Manor Inn, a National Historic Landmark, the house retains its antebellum allure, with original features that include a black-marble fireplace and a 2,000-square-foot wraparound veranda on three sides. Doorknobs on the original doors are about a foot lower than you'd expect them to be, and one guest suite includes stairs to the square cupola, which is set up as a sitting room.

BROADWAY BY THE SEA

Why is this theater company called an opera company?

A courtyard strung with lights leads to the Highfield Theatre, a historic playhouse reimagined from the stables and carriage house of the bygone-era mansion next door. This Falmouth estate is where CLOC, a music theater company and training ground for young performers, takes the stage each summer.

You're likely to catch some up-and-coming stars, as many CLOC alums make the leap to stage and screen, including Broadway actors Analisa Leaming (*School of Rock* and *The King and I*), Geno Carr (*Come from Away*) and Kaitlyn Jackson (*Anastasia* national tour), to name just a few.

While CLOC is an acronym for College Light Opera Company, it's not actually an opera company. "College and opera are two things that people don't like about the name," said Executive and Artistic Director Mark A. Pearson. "Most people don't want to see college kids doing opera."

While the actors, musicians, designers, and technicians are indeed college students, CLOC selects "the best of the best" from highly competitive theater and music programs, Pearson said. And while the company, founded in 1969, has roots in operetta, it has since evolved into musical theater. Students who land a coveted spot have the chance to work with acclaimed directors and music directors, such as Grammy- and Tony-nominated stage and screen actor Bryce Pinkham, who directed a 2019 show.

The company presents nine shows each summer—six performances per week—split between three golden-age musicals,

THE COLLEGE LIGHT OPERA COMPANY (CLOC)

WHAT: A preprofessional music theater company

WHERE: Highfield Theatre, 58 Highfield Dr., Falmouth

COST: $40

PRO TIP: Meet the cast: the actors greet fans after every Tuesday-night and Wednesday matinee performance.

Top: *Catch the stars of tomorrow at CLOC. Photo by James Humphrey.* Inset: *Not a cookie-cutter theater: Note the curved black railings at the Highfield Theatre's door—they were used to tie up horses in the 19th century. Photo by Linda Humphrey*

three modern musicals, and three classical pieces. There's even a sought-after family musical such as *Mary Poppins* or *Cinderella*. Perhaps the out-of-place name is just part of this company's charm.

Three hundred actor-singer-dancers vied for 24 spots in the 2022 CLOC vocal company.

THE HIGH LIFE

Where can you take a cooking class in a haunted mansion?

Ghost hunting isn't listed on Highfield Hall's vast menu of activities and events, which range from cooking classes to jazz concerts to a costume contest for dogs.

Still, this Gilded Age mansion in Falmouth, now a vibrant cultural center and art museum, is said to be haunted by one of its original residents. Visitors have reported sightings of a woman looking out a second-floor window toward the garden, and—late at night—the sound of high heels tapping down the main staircase.

Once the scene of lavish parties, the English-style country manor built in 1878 was the summer home of Boston's Bebee family. A fun-loving and quirky bunch, they were known to weigh their guests before and after their festive dinners. (President Grover Cleveland was once a dinner guest; no word on whether he weighed in.)

J. Arthur Beebe and his daughter Emily were booked on the *Titanic* but missed the boat. Less than a year later, Emily died by suicide at a Boston hotel. An exhibit at Highfield Hall details the full story.

HIGHFIELD HALL

WHAT: Gilded Age mansion turned cultural center

WHERE: 56 Highfield Dr., Falmouth

COST: $10 adults, $8 seniors; children and military free. Docent-led estate tours are offered free with admission and are held on the first and third Sundays of each month from June to October.

PRO TIP: Lobster on the Lawn at the castle-like Saint Barnabas's Episcopal Church, built for the Bebee family in 1889, is a fun weekly event. Step inside, and you'll see that each stained-glass window is dedicated to a Bebee family member.

Top: *Does a ghost descend this staircase after dark?* Bottom: *The mansion has 15 fireplaces, each with a different style of mantle. Photos by Linda Humphrey*

After decades of neglect, a dilapidated Highfield was slated for the wrecking ball in 1994. The mansion's stables had been redesigned into the Highfield Theatre in 1947—with the Bebee's pet cemetery paved over to become the theater's parking lot—and the town had demolished a second Bebee mansion on the estate in 1977. A local group rallied to save Highfield Hall, which finally opened in 2006, a rare surviving example of Stick-style Queen Anne architecture in the Northeast.

CARIBBEAN ON THE CAPE

Where can you savor the flavors of Jamaica on a Cape Cod farm?

If it's Wednesday night in the summertime on Coonamessett Farm, then it's time to dig into some jerk chicken, mango salsa, and jalapeño corn bread, washed down with some lemonade or homemade ginger beer. Or maybe sample some tender greens called callaloo or spicy pepper pot soup. These are among the bountiful selections at the Jamaican Buffet, a popular weekly tradition at the 20-acre farm in East Falmouth since 2006.

So how did a Cape Cod farm, which is also known among locals as a place to pick your own produce or hold a wedding, become a spot to enjoy Jamaican specialties and dance to a steel drum band? Owner Ron Smolowitz, who purchased the 20-acre farm back in 1982, had long offered farm-to-table dinners in a spacious pavilion overlooking the fields. As the events ended, the Jamaican kitchen staff would sit down to enjoy their own preparations, the spicy aromas drawing looks of envy and curiosity among the diners. It became obvious to Smolowitz that Jamaica-themed events would go over well.

He also knew it would serve another purpose—boosting the morale of the immigrant kitchen workers. "It forms a direct connection between our customers and staff," he said. "To me this is the main reason for the local farm, a celebration of community and self-reliance."

Coonamessett Farm forges community ties in a variety of ways, including through a popular membership club where families pay a monthly fee to pick their own fruits and vegetables as well as mingle with the resident ducks, donkeys, goats, and alpacas. The farm also offers tours that include demonstrations of its hydroponic and aquaculture production. Fall is an especially busy time, filled with Halloween celebrations and Harvest Weekends featuring

Coonamessett Farm hosts Jamaican buffets on Wednesday nights in the summer.

pumpkin picking, hayrides, and live music. Visitors can also pop into the Farm Stand, which sells everything from local honey to alpaca-wool clothing and baskets from Ghana, and the Peck O'Dirt Bakery, which has sweet and savory baked treats, including vegan and gluten-free options.

JAMAICA NIGHTS

WHAT: Jamaican Buffet at Coonamessett Farm

WHERE: 277 Hatchville Rd., East Falmouth

COST: $25

PRO TIP: For more tastes of Jamaica, try the Jerk Cafe (thejerkcafe.com) in Yarmouth. Glenroy Burke, also known as Chef Shrimpy, serves up jerk chicken and pork, banana fritters, and other specialties from his homeland.

For more than three decades, Jamaican chefs and cooks have been coming to Cape Cod through the H-2B visa program, which provides a pathway for foreign workers toward temporary nonagricultural jobs. At least 500 Jamaicans are estimated to be working in local restaurant kitchens, often bringing Caribbean flavors to traditional Cape menus.

ON THE LOOKOUT

Where will you find crowd-free seaside views and a *Titanic* exhibit?

This mile-long seaside trek with three beaches along Quissett Harbor and Buzzards Bay leads to an island-like overlook with knockout views. Once part of a private resort owned by the Carey family for nearly a century, the 12-acre nature preserve known as the Knob opened to the public, dogs in tow, in the 1970s.

The trails begin at Quissett Harbor, brimming with boats. But first, a warning: there are only about 20 parking spots on Quissett Harbor Road. Try your luck—there are no facilities here, so no one lingers for long—go early, or get dropped off.

As you set out alongside a harborside beach, Little Sandy, to the trail lined with beach-plum bushes, you'll reach a fork. Veer right for the overlook or to hit the Caribbean-clear water of Buzzards Bay at dog-friendly Crescent Beach.

Turn left for the Harbor Cliff Trail, which will bring you to the Inner Harbor Overlook and the harborside Fisherman's Beach. Once out of the woods, a narrow spit of land heads to the main

THE KNOB/CORNELIA CAREY SANCTUARY

WHAT: A 12-acre nature preserve with three beaches and an overlook with views of Buzzards Bay

WHERE: 48 Quissett Harbor Rd., Woods Hole

COST: Free

PRO TIP: Pull up a map of the Knob at savebuzzardsbay.org.

This historic seaside village seems an unlikely place to learn about the discovery of the *Titanic*. Uncover the connection at the Woods Hole Oceanographic Institute's Ocean Science Discovery Center, at 15 School Street.

Top: *The Knob is open from 8 a.m. to sunset. Photo by Jon Miksis.* Inset: *Kids flock to the interactive* Titanic *exhibit at the Ocean Science Discovery Center. Photo by Linda Humphrey*

attraction: the lookout where you'll catch sight of the Elizabeth Islands to the south, New Bedford to the west, and the canal entrance to the north.

The après-beach scene here involves lobster or fish tacos at the California-surf-shack-meets-New-England-seafood-shack called Quicks Hole Taqueria. (Order on the Toast app to avoid the line.) For us, opening day here has always marked the official start of summer.

HOW THE COWS CAME HOME

Where can you find a magnificent stone edifice that provided safe passage for dairy cows?

Back in the early 20th century, when Cape Cod was home to numerous dairy farms, farmers faced a dilemma with the increasing number of highways and railroad tracks getting in their way. How were they to move their cows safely between grazing pastures to watering holes without encountering pesky cars or trains along the way? The solution was to build cow tunnels, a means of giving bovines their own passageways underneath highways and railroad tracks.

A few of these cow tunnels remain on the Cape, the most remarkable of which is a structure of finely crafted stonework reminiscent of a medieval fortress. The tunnel, which is known as Dry Bridge, was built in 1928 and runs under Race Lane near the Cape Cod Airfield in Marston Mills. It enabled the dairy cows to easily travel from their pastures to the waters of Mystic Lake. No longer in service for cows (most Cape dairy farms were out of business by the 1960s due to health regulations and skyrocketing land prices), the tunnel today is primarily used by hikers taking a shortcut to Mystic Lake along the Danforth Trail, part of the Danforth Recreation Area.

Another remaining cow tunnel, this one not as elaborate, can be found beneath the Shining Sea Bikeway, a bike path created

Cow tunnels are just a few of many curiosities lurking in the woods and fields of Cape Cod. Another is Chamber Rock, aka Sacrifice Rock, in Bournedale off Chamber Rock Road, supposedly a place of human sacrifice in ancient times.

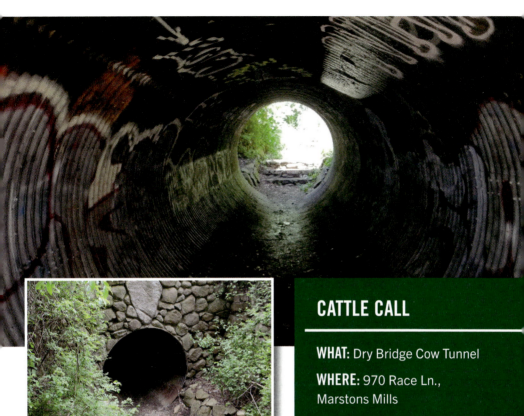

The Dry Bridge Cow Tunnel is no longer a shortcut for cows but remains an intriguing curiosity.

CATTLE CALL

WHAT: Dry Bridge Cow Tunnel

WHERE: 970 Race Ln., Marstons Mills

COST: Free

PRO TIP: Visit the nearby Cape Cod Airfield, a 1920s airfield with grass runways and a quaint windmill. It offers biplane rides, skydiving lessons, and, for the less intrepid, a picnic area from which you can watch the planes and skydivers. Rumor has it that Amelia Earhart once landed there.

from a once-bustling train track, which cuts through the grounds of Bourne Farm in West Falmouth. After checking out the tunnel, there's plenty to explore at the farm, which is part of the Salt Pond Areas Bird Sanctuaries and offers walking trails through meadows and woodlands. Its bountiful pumpkin fields are a popular family attraction during fall.

TALE OF TWO CAPES

What is the connection between Cape Verde and Cape Cod?

Cape Verde, a volcanic island nation and former Portuguese colony 385 miles off the west coast of Africa, may be a world away from Cape Cod, but there are links between the two vastly different places. After drought and famine decimated nearly a quarter of the population in the 19th century, many Cape Verdeans, who are usually a mix of Portuguese and African ancestry, immigrated to Rhode Island and Massachusetts to work in the whaling industry.

When the whaling industry waned, many Cape Verdeans who had settled on Cape Cod found work in the cranberry bogs in the days before cranberry harvesting became mechanized. "The Wampanoags taught us how to pick cranberries and start our own bogs," said Barbara Burgo, a third-generation Cape resident of Cape Verdean descent, in an interview with the *Cape Cod Times.* "We worked alongside

Barnstable's Eugenia Fortes Beach, a serene stretch of sand laden with seashells and beach grass, is named for a Cape Verdean immigrant who worked as a housekeeper and cranberry harvester and eventually became a civil rights activist on behalf of African Americans.

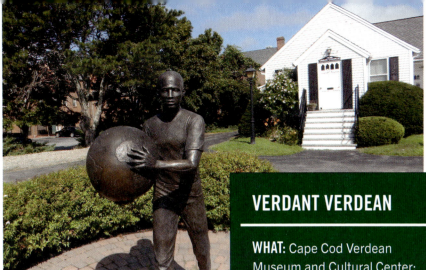

The Zion Union Heritage Museum has an impressive collection of Cape Verdean art.

VERDANT VERDEAN

WHAT: Cape Cod Verdean Museum and Cultural Center; Zion Union Heritage Museum

WHERE: 67 Davisville Rd., East Falmouth; 276 North St., Hyannis

COST: Cape Cod Verdean: $30 annual membership; Zion Union Heritage: $5 adults, $3 children 10–17, under 10 free

PRO TIP: Cape Verdean dishes such as jagacida (known as jag), a mix of rice, beans, and sausage, and caldo de peixe, Cape Verdean braised bluefish, are sometimes found on menus at Cape Cod restaurants.

Finnish people who came to Cape Cod in the late 1800s and 1900s."

Burgo is curator and cofounder of the Cape Cod Verdean Museum and Cultural Center, which is located in Emerald House, a historic farmhouse in East Falmouth filled with artifacts and memorabilia from the daily life of Cape Verdean immigrants. The center offers events such as cooking classes, concerts, language classes, and lectures as well as exhibits on art and history. It also maintains a "Sister School Project" between the Falmouth Public Schools and a school in Cape Verde.

Also celebrating Cape Verdean culture, along with African American history on Cape Cod, is the Zion Union Heritage Museum in Hyannis, which provides tours, exhibits, and special events honoring Black History Month in February. The museum has an impressive art collection, including a stunning bronze statue of a life-sized African American/Cape Verdean man holding a huge globe with his left hand on Africa and his fingers pointing toward America.

CAFÉ WITH A CONSCIENCE

Where can you browse for a good book, sip a fresh brew, enjoy a plant-based meal, and be part of an ethical vision?

In the East Main Street area of downtown Hyannis is a combination bookstore, coffee roastery, and vegan café that is more than the sum of its parts. Called Bread + Roses, it reflects the vision of owner Nathan Herschler, who jettisoned a legal and public policy career with international animal welfare organizations to focus on making a difference on the community level, especially with such issues as food waste, food deserts, and food insecurity.

All three of these food issues are prevalent in the Bread + Roses locale, according to Herschler, who says that Hyannis, like many other upscale tourist destinations, has a two-tiered economy in which immigrant workers struggle to find affordable housing and, because they often lack cars, convenient access to quality groceries. To address the latter problem, he plans to open a fresh-food market near the café that will include a zero-waste component, event space, and a commercial kitchen for community use that can serve as an incubator for small culinary businesses.

In the meantime, Bread + Roses has become a popular place to sip fresh-ground, single-origin coffee and peruse a menu of tasty, chef-prepared vegan dishes made with ingredients sourced from local farmers and purveyors. There's plenty to tempt even non-vegans, including sweet potato fries, burritos stuffed with crispy oyster mushrooms, and toast topped with spreads like avocado and sun-

LABOR OF LOVE

WHAT: Bread + Roses

WHERE: 302 Main St., Hyannis

COST: $3–$18

PRO TIP: On the go? Bread + Roses offers packaged goodies such as strawberry overnight oats and protein bites with maple-sweetened nuts and seeds.

Bread + Roses is a place to find books, food, and good causes. Photos by Maria Lenhart

dried tomatoes or a tangy-sweet concoction of mangos and plantains. Patrons can also Pay It Forward by donating a coffee drink or premade sandwich to the local community.

Right off the café, the bookstore offers cozy alcoves where customers can curl up on sofas or armchairs with their latest find. Its shelves are stocked with new and used books, including bestsellers, literary classics, books on Cape Cod history, and travel ideas along with curated picks from the staff. Not surprisingly, there are also vegan cookbooks and books pertaining to labor history and justice.

On occasion, Bread + Roses is also a gathering spot for fundraisers and entertainment, offering concerts by local musicians and appearances by authors and historians. These recently included a talk by historian Bruce Watson on the 1912 Bread and Roses Strike, which took place in Lowell, Massachusetts, at a textile mill employing women and children.

"Bread + Roses is a hybrid bookstore-café that was born to nourish your body, enrich your mind, and celebrate your soul," Herschel said.

The term Bread and Roses, which became a slogan for social justice, was first coined by Helen Todd, a women's suffrage activist, who in a 1910 speech called for bread (symbolizing home and security) and roses (symbolizing the arts and nature) to be the birthright of every child born in the United States.

PLAY BALL!

Where can you see baseball superstars of tomorrow playing on local ball fields throughout the Cape?

Attending a game on a late summer afternoon on a grassy local field and hearing the thwack of balls hitting wooden bats is a long-standing tradition courtesy of the Cape Cod Baseball League (CCBL). It's among the premier collegiate summer baseball leagues in the nation, and 1,600 former participants have gone on to play in the major leagues. The CCBL offers a 44-game regular season that extends from mid-June through mid-August, along with a postseason of playoff games. It has two divisions with a total of 10 teams located in Bourne, Brewster, Chatham, Cotuit, Falmouth, Harwich, Hyannis, Orleans, Wareham, and Yarmouth/Dennis.

The nonprofit, largely volunteer-run CCBL recruits players and coaches from across the US representing all NCAA college divisions. Local families host the collegiate players in their homes. Among current and recent major leaguers who played in the CCBL are Aaron Judge (New York Yankees), Chris Sale (Boston Red Sox), Alek Manoah (Toronto Blue Jays), Pete Alonso (New York Mets), Kyle Schwarber (Philadelphia Phillies), Aaron Nola (Philadelphia Phillies), Adley Rutschman (Baltimore Orioles), Shane Bieber (Cleveland Guardians), Corbin Burnes (Milwaukee Brewers), and Will Smith (Los Angeles Dodgers).

Officially formed in 1923, the CCBL's roots extend deep into the 19th century. In the 1860s, baseball teams representing several

---

The infamous donut burger, in which a meat patty is paired with a donut serving as the bun, is said to have originated at games played by the Yarmouth/Dennis Red Sox at Red Wilson Field. Several variations with jelly, cream, or glazed donuts are on the menu.

The Cape Cod Baseball League has long been a favorite local pastime. Top left image courtesy of Massachusetts Office of Travel and Tourism

A LEAGUE OF THEIR OWN

WHAT: Cape Cod Baseball League

WHERE: For a schedule of games, visit capecodbaseball.org

COST: Free (a small donation is encouraged)

PRO TIP: Check out the CCBL Hall of Fame and Museum with its exhibits and memorabilia honoring past players, coaches, and others. It's located on the lower level of the John F. Kennedy Hyannis Museum at 397 Main St. in Hyannis.

Cape Cod towns were competing against each other. By the late 19th century, an annual championship baseball tournament was held at the Barnstable County Fair each fall, an event that continued well into the 20th century with teams representing towns from Cape Cod and the larger region. As interest grew, plans were made to create a formal Cape Cod league.

The CCBL has since made its way into the world of film and books. It was the backdrop for the 2001 romantic comedy *Summer Catch* starring Freddie Prinze Jr. and Jessica Biel, and also the setting for several mystery novels, including *Second Law* and *Death at the Edge of the Diamond*, by Falmouth author Paul Raymer.

ICE CREAM IN CAMELOT

Which ice cream shop on the Cape has long been a Kennedy family favorite?

Perhaps not too surprising in a summertime destination, Cape Cod seems to have as many places to get ice cream as it does grains of sand. The oldest and most iconic of all these sweet-treat purveyors is Four Seas, a former blacksmith shop in Centerville where generations of Cape Cod families have gotten their daily scoop since 1934.

Among those local families are the Kennedys, whose famous compound is in nearby Hyannis. Not only have members of the Kennedy clan frequently been spotted buying cones at Four Seas over the years, but JFK had the ice cream flown down to the White House during his administration in the early 1960s. Jacqueline Kennedy Onassis requested that its peach ice cream be served at her daughter Caroline's wedding rehearsal dinner for 100 guests held at the Hyannisport Club in 1986.

COLD SPOT

WHAT: Four Seas Ice Cream

WHERE: 360 S Main St., Centerville

COST: Ice cream is $5 and up.

PRO TIP: Also iconic is Ben & Bill's Chocolate Emporium, with shops in Falmouth and on Martha's Vineyard in Oak Bluffs, where the adventurous can try the lobster ice cream.

Four Seas Ice Cream is most famous for its fresh peach ice cream served at a Kennedy wedding. Photo courtesy of Massachusetts Office of Travel & Tourism

Ben & Bill's Chocolate Emporium in Falmouth. Photo by Linda Humphrey

"Peach was always her favorite," Richard Warren, owner of Four Seas at the time, told United Press International regarding Jackie's choice. "The Kennedys have been coming here for three generations."

Today visitors and locals alike still crowd into the shop, which has a counter with stools and a small dining room serving not only ice cream desserts but sandwiches, lobster rolls, and other lunch fare. Along with peach, which is available only when fresh peaches are in season, signature ice cream flavors include black raspberry, cranberry, gingerbread, peanut butter chocolate chip, and penuche pecan, an old-fashioned brown-sugar flavor based on a New England recipe.

All of the ice cream at Four Seas is still made by hand at a single machine in the back room of the little building. During peak season, current owners Doug and Peggy Warren and their staff will make as many as 680 gallons per day.

The name Four Seas, which was taken from the poem "Cape Cod Calls" by Mabel E. Phinney, refers to the four bodies of water surrounding the Cape: the Atlantic Ocean, Buzzards Bay, Cape Cod Bay, and Nantucket Sound.

THE VERY WITCHING TIME OF NIGHT

Where can you hunt for ghosts with a paranormal researcher?

Have you ever wanted to wander an ancient cemetery on a foggy night, reading tombstones by flashlight and speaking to the dead? Here's your chance.

It was nearly Halloween as our group approached the lichen-covered 18th- and 19th-century gravestones of Cobb's Hill Cemetery in Barnstable Village. At the entrance—known as Death's Doorway—our Ghost Hunters Tour leader, Derek Bartlett, pointed out the iron fence. Colonial Americans believed that ghosts could not pass through iron, and they avoided entering the graveyard along with the dead, which would curse you to die within a year. Pallbearers would slide coffins on two pillars at Death's Doorway to others already within the cemetery.

Bartlett handed out EVP (electronic voice phenomenon) recorders, and we prowled the burial ground with flashlights, crickets chirping, asking questions at tombstones, hoping (or not) to pick up a response on the recorders.

A paranormal researcher who has lectured at universities, Bartlett is not your typical ghost-walk leader. His tours are interactive, which proved to be especially fun for the bachelorette party in our group. As the rest of us kept our distance, Bartlett asked the bride-to-be to walk up to the spooky Barnstable House and pound on the door three times.

There were no replies on our recorders that night, but Bartlett played a recording from a few months back. A couple had visited

What are those tiny headstones? They're actually footstones, marking the foot of the grave.

BARNSTABLE VILLAGE GHOST HUNTERS TOUR

WHAT: Three-hour walking tour to haunted sites in Barnstable Village, including Cobb's Hill Cemetery

WHERE: Starts and ends at the Old Jail, 3353 Main St. (Rte. 6A), Barnstable

COST: $20

PRO TIP: In addition to the three-hour Ghost Hunters Tour, Derek Bartlett leads two-hour Haunted & History Tours. Call or text 508-241-1151 for more information or to reserve your spot.

This one-of-a-kind tour will take you to Cobb's Hill Cemetery after dark.
Top: *Death's Doorway. Photos by Linda Humphrey*

the graves of Sarah and Lily, ages 7 and 11, a twirling pinwheel set before each headstone.

"Okay, girls, we're going now," the wife said. The reply was so faint—a whisper—that we had to pass the recorder around to hear it. The words—eliciting screams from the bachelorette party—were *Get out.* You've been warned.

VONNEGUT'S SAAB STORY

Where and why did the author Kurt Vonnegut shift gears to run a car dealership?

In 1952 an aspiring novelist named Kurt Vonnegut Jr. ditched his job as a public relations executive for General Electric and moved to the mid-Cape town of Barnstable with his wife and six kids. It was there that he would eventually write some of his best-known works, including *Slaughterhouse-Five* and *Cat's Cradle*.

Before he struck literary gold, however, Vonnegut found himself short of the funds needed to support his large family. In 1957, fascinated with the innovative new Saab automobile, he set up Saab Cape Cod, one of the first dealerships for the Swedish imports in the US, in an old stone garage on Route 6A, now part of the Old King's Highway Historical District in West Barnstable. Vonnegut soon found the business hardgoing, partly because the cars required a new quart of oil with every tank of gas, which made them a hard sell. The building still stands and can be seen from the highway, although it hasn't been a car dealership for decades.

Commenting on the short-lived venture in an essay written in 2004, Vonnegut quipped that "I now believe my failure as a dealer so long ago explains what would otherwise remain a deep mystery: Why the Swedes have never given me a Nobel Prize for literature."

Not only did Vonnegut go on to achieve literary success, he became one of Barnstable's leading citizens, serving on the board of the Sturgis Library and as president of the Barnstable

VEHICLE VENTURE

WHAT: Vonnegut Saab

WHERE: 1611 Main St. (Rte. 6A), West Barnstable

COST: None

PRO TIP: While exploring Route 6A, enjoy some fair-trade coffee and house-made pastries in a living room–like setting at Nirvana Coffee Company in Barnstable Village.

This stone building once served as Kurt Vonnegut's Saab dealership.

Comedy Club before moving to New York City in 1971. In 1964 he wrote a sardonic essay about the town called "You've Never Been to Barnstable." He noted its steadfast resistance to development, declaring that "all the anachronistic, mildly xenophobic, charming queernesses of Barnstable Village might entitle it to be called 'Last Stronghold of the True Cape Codders.'"

Just off Route 6A in West Barnstable is Sandy Neck, a six-mile-long barrier beach of vast dunes, maritime forests, and salt marsh with a network of trails. It's a haven for rare birds and wildlife.

CATCH A SHOW— OR A GHOST

Why is this century-old (haunted) theater called a comedy club?

The play was going well until a woman in a Victorian dress suddenly appeared onstage. The actors broke character and froze—until, seconds later, she vanished.

This Victorian ghost has appeared twice at the century-old Barnstable Comedy Club (BCC), which is not a stand-up comedy club but the oldest community theater group on the Cape and one of the oldest in the country. Founded in 1922 and housed in the 1915 Village Hall, the theater's illustrious past includes a collaboration in the '50s and '60s with Kurt Vonnegut Jr., who once performed there in a leopard skin. The BCC appears in Vonnegut's work as well, under the guise of the North Crawford Mask and Wig Club.

True to its name, the all-volunteer BCC tends toward lighthearted, often G-rated fare, staging one musical and three plays each year. Off-season travelers, take note: shows run from November to May. Summer brings a bustling musical-theater camp, Cape Cod Kids on Broadway, to the Village Hall.

THE BARNSTABLE COMEDY CLUB

WHAT: Century-old community theater

WHERE: 3171 Main St., Barnstable

COST: $30, $28 for seniors and students

PRO TIP: Arrive early, or you will be stuck in the back row. All seating is first come, first served.

Kurt Vonnegut Jr. gave the BCC permission to perform any of his plays for free, in perpetuity.

The Village Hall, home to the Barnstable Comedy Club, dates to 1915 and its ghost to 1940. Photo by Linda Humphrey

The antique theater is also a stop on Derek Bartlett's ghost tour. The Victorian—who surfaced before audiences in 1940 and 1970—is a residual haunting, Bartlett said, leftover energy from the past that repeats itself and never changes, like a movie clip. Is she due to appear onstage again?

A STORIED PAST

Is the Sturgis Library the oldest public library in America—or not?

A stately fixture on the Old King's Highway (Route 6A) in Barnstable, the Sturgis Library—at least part of it—has a history dating back almost to Pilgrim days, when it was built as a meetinghouse and residence for the Reverend John Lothrop in 1644. It didn't morph into a library, however, until a Lothrop descendant named William Sturgis, an adventurous sea captain and fur trader in his youth, willed the old family home, designed in the classic "half-Cape" style, along with $15,000 in bonds, for that purpose. The Sturgis Library opened in 1867 with 1,300 volumes, many of them from its benefactor's own collection.

So even though it is not the oldest public library in America, the Sturgis does claim to be the oldest building in the country housing a public library. It also happens to be the oldest structure still standing in America where religious services were regularly held. While its age and inclusion on the National Register of Historic Places is impressive, that's hardly the only reason the Sturgis Library is a worthwhile stop for researchers and booklovers.

Its most intriguing feature is the Lothrop Room, the original meetinghouse room at the front of the building, which retains historic Cape charm with its pumpkin-colored wide-board floors, antique furnishings, and beamed ceiling. A first edition of *Moby-Dick* and Reverend Lothrop's Bible, with repairs to its ancient pages, are among the treasures on display in the room.

William Sturgis was an advocate for the rights of the indigenous people of the Pacific Northwest, with whom he had traded during his years as a young merchant sea captain in the early 19th century.

The Sturgis Library, which contains an original copy of Moby-Dick *and other treasures, has roots as a meetinghouse in the Pilgrim era. Photo by Maria Lenhart*

LITERARY LEGACY

WHAT: Sturgis Library

WHERE: 3090 Main St., Barnstable

COST: Free

PRO TIP: Be sure and check out the library's impressive lineup of special events, which includes everything from yoga sessions to literary festivals, held throughout the year.

Far more than a museum, however, the Sturgis is very much a working library, with over 65,000 volumes and many special collections pertaining to Cape Cod history. These include the Lothrop Genealogy Collection, which draws genealogists from around the country to examine their connections to Cape Cod, and the Kittredge Maritime Collections, notable for its concentration on Cape Cod sea captains and vessels.

COLONIAL GRAFFITI

Where can you step inside the country's oldest (haunted) Colonial jail?

Looking for a creepy place that Harry Potter might encounter? This is it. Reputed to be the oldest surviving wooden jail in the country and one of America's most haunted places, the 1690 Old Jail looks like something you'd find on a movie set.

If the exterior appears fake, the interior—with its original locks, etchings, and graffiti—is unsettling. Carved into the wall's wood planks, you'll find a sketch of a ship and a message reading "W. Bartlett 13d October 1698 and 27d he was let out." A rickety loft holds two confinement cells.

While the well-off managed to avoid this dungeon by posting bail or bribing the sheriff, less-fortunate prisoners awaiting trial—debtors, fortune tellers, runaways, unruly servants, pirates, and even children—were thrown into windowless cells so crowded that they had to sleep by taking turns.

Present-day ghost hunters, chief among them paranormal investigator Derek Bartlett, have reported chilling encounters here. Bartlett once felt an unseen hand on his back—and then felt the entity reach its arms around him in a

OLD JAIL (OLD GAOL)

WHAT: Oldest wooden jail in the country, built in 1690. Reputed to be one of America's most haunted places.

WHERE: 3353 Main St., Barnstable

COST: $5 donation

PRO TIP: Wish you could spend the night here? Bartlett offers jail stays from 9 p.m. to 1 a.m.

Nantucket's creepy old prison on Vestal Street, built in 1805, is open for tours as well. Tales of jailbreaks include that of a 15-year-old boy who crawled out the chimney.

hug. A colleague took photos, on display at the jail, which revealed that Bartlett's sweatshirt had been grabbed from behind and pulled, causing the sensation of a hug.

Bartlett's tour takes thrill-seekers to the jailhouse after dark, where he snaps off the lights and calls up its ghosts. Listening to his stories in the dark, people will sometimes scream, Bartlett said, claiming that something has grabbed them.

The Old Jail includes a horrifying exhibit on Colonial-era punishments. Photo by Linda Humphrey

THE PIRATE, THE WITCH, AND THE *WHYDAH*

Where will you find the only pirate treasure ever discovered?

The legend of the *Whydah*, a pirate ship that wrecked off the coast of Wellfleet, includes treasure, a witch, and JFK Jr. It begins with a love story.

In 1714, Englishman Sam Bellamy sailed to Wellfleet, where he fell for blonde teenager Maria "Goody" Hallett, a sought-after beauty from a well-to-do family. Her parents forbade their marriage, so Bellamy sailed off in search of fortune.

By 1717, 28-year-old Bellamy had become the richest pirate in history. He headed back to the Cape as captain of the *Whydah*, a captured slave vessel stocked with booty from more than 50 plundered ships. Hit by a storm just 500 feet from the beach, the *Whydah* sank, flinging Bellamy and about 140 pirates into the ocean.

Three hundred years later, in 1984, underwater explorer Barry Clifford and his first mate, John F. Kennedy Jr., discovered the wreck. The underwater excavation is still ongoing, with six pirate skeletons uncovered in 2021.

Clifford launched the Whydah Pirate Museum in West Yarmouth to showcase thousands of salvaged artifacts, including a treasure chest heaped with coins, the only pirate treasure ever found. You'll walk through a replica of the *Whydah* complete with Disney-like moving figures and sound effects such as tavern music,

---

Most pirates didn't know how to swim, but two managed to make it to shore alive, where they were soon captured and locked up in the Old Jail to await trial.

The Whydah, *a captured slave vessel, was stocked with booty from more than 50 plundered ships. Photo by Ben Nugent*

creaking boards, and ocean waves. Exhibits sketch out life on slave ships (slaves were forced to dance on deck for exercise) and pirate ships (FYI, walking the plank and maps to buried treasure are myths).

The museum doesn't cover Maria's fate, but legend has it that she was banished for an out-of-wedlock pregnancy. She was locked in Barnstable's Old Jail but managed to escape—most likely because the jailor took pity on her—which led the townspeople to label her the Witch of Wellfleet.

WHYDAH PIRATE MUSEUM

WHAT: 300-year-old pirate ship exhibition

WHERE: 674 MA-28, West Yarmouth

COST: $17

PRO TIP: The nearby Skipper Chowder House is one of Cape Cod's oldest waterfront restaurants, established in 1936.

CRUISING THE OLD KING'S HIGHWAY

Where will you find rows of century-old sea captains' houses that stretch for over a mile?

Take a break from beach-hopping for this road trip that's been called one of the world's most scenic drives by *National Geographic* and "the most appealing stretch of America I know" by *Smithsonian* magazine writer Jonathan Sandell. The Old King's Highway—also known as Route 6A—is the country's largest contiguous historic district, a National Historic Landmark, and a National Scenic Byway.

Once a Native American trail and stagecoach route lined with rollicking taverns, this iconic road winds past architecture from four centuries and travels all the way from Bourne to Provincetown. (Note that, as you reach Eastham, 6A merges into Route 6 and then reemerges in North Truro.)

At Yarmouth Port, stroll the village to take in the Captains' Mile, a time capsule of more than 50 sea captains' homes, all marked with black-and-gold schooner plaques. Step into Hallet's Store, an 1889 soda shop complete with stained-glass windows and vintage signs, for a dose of nostalgia along with your milkshake. Actually, don't order a milkshake—they're called frappes in these parts (pronounced "fraps"), as fourth-generation owner Charlie

---

The Church of the New Jerusalem—now Thatcher Hall—followed the philosophy of 18th-century theologian Emmanuel Swedenborg, who claimed to have communicated with the spiritual world. Swedenborg never intended to start a church, but many, grieving the losses of the Civil War, were drawn to his teachings.

Left: *Yarmouth Port's Thatcher Hall was built as a Swedenborgian Church in 1870. Photo by Linda Humphrey.* Right: *An array of cafés, historic inns, sea captains' homes, and artisan shops line the Old King's Highway. Photo courtesy of Massachusetts Office of Travel & Tourism*

THE OLD KING'S HIGHWAY

WHAT: One of the most scenic drives on the planet

WHERE: Route 6A runs from Bourne to Provincetown.

COST: Free

PRO TIP: Pick up or download a map of the Captains' Mile from the Yarmouth Historical Society, hsoy.org/thecaptainsmile.

Clark will remind you. Built as the local pharmacy—note the original oak apothecary drawers—the shop added a soda fountain in the 1930s, when you could also pick up a five-cent Coke and your newspaper. Today's menu also includes clam chowder and sandwiches.

Just up the street, Thatcher Hall, a Carpenter Gothic–style church turned cultural center, has been called "the most significant historic public structure of its period on Cape Cod" by architect Sara Jane Porter. Note the original 1870 stained-glass windows, frescoed walls, and pews carved from now-rare American chestnut wood.

SOMEWHERE, BEYOND THE SEA, PART ONE

Why is there a car at the bottom of Hathaway's Pond?

Surrounded by pitch pine and oak trees, more than 800 freshwater kettle ponds are scattered throughout the Cape. Many of these under-the-radar natural pools are reached only by hiking or biking, while others offer just a handful of parking spots or require resident stickers. But gate monitors leave by 5 p.m., and most town beach offices sell visitor parking passes. Here are a few—of many—dreamy swimming spots worth seeking out on a hot summer's day. You might even find an old-time rope swing.

Scuba divers pull on wet suits and plunge into Hathaway's Pond, its water transparent to 20 feet below the surface. A popular dive training and certification site thanks to its clear water, this Barnstable pond is touted for its sunken wrecks: a cabin cruiser and a 1985 Saab. While the boat was sunk about 30 feet below the surface for dive practice, the car is reputed to have been stolen and driven onto the frozen pond, where it eventually fell through the ice.

With midsummer water temperatures reaching 84 degrees, Hathaway's bustles with swimmers and families as well. There's a roped-off swim area for kids, lifeguards, and a bathhouse.

At Nickerson State Park in Brewster, swimmers flock to Flax Pond. Parking costs $8 if you have a Massachusetts license plate; nonresidents pay $30. This 1,900-acre park with eight ponds in all—

HATHAWAY'S POND

WHAT: Kettle pond for scuba divers (and swimmers)

WHERE: 1431 Phinney's Ln., Barnstable

COST: $25 to park before 5 p.m.

PRO TIP: Capecodbeaches.net lists information—including parking fees, sticker requirements, facilities, and typical crowd sizes—for most beaches and ponds.

Dive in! Hathaway's Pond is a great place to explore, whether on or under the water. Photo by Linda Humphrey

once the estate of Roland Nickerson, a Chatham native who founded the First National Bank of Chicago—also offers 418 campsites.

There's another Flax Pond in Dennis, with parking just off Setucket Road. Bring your dog and try the rope swing, no parking sticker needed.

Just to confuse you, some of the kettle ponds across the Cape have the same names: Flax, Great, and Long.

SUMMER PLAYDATES

What role did Cape Cod play in America's entertainment history?

While lobster rolls, quaint towns, and beaches are an undeniable part of Cape Cod's allure for summer visitors, so are the performing arts. Since the late 1800s, impresarios have eyed the Cape as a spot to establish theatrical companies, one that could draw audiences and a wealth of talent. Many of these early theaters, among them the Falmouth Playhouse, once called the most beautiful summer theater in America, and the Provincetown Players, a launching pad for young Eugene O'Neill, are long gone, but others are alive and well.

Getting top billing is the Cape Playhouse, started when a California impresario named Raymond Moore, who had originally planned to start a theater in Provincetown but decided it was too remote, paid $200 for an old Unitarian meetinghouse in Dennis. The theater, which staged its first play in 1927, became known as the "Cradle of Stars" because of the Broadway and Hollywood luminaries who got their start there. Along with Humphrey Bogart, Henry Fonda, and Gregory Peck, these included Bette Davis, who served as an usher before getting her big break when an actress fell ill. The prestigious company, which bills itself as "America's Favorite Summer Theater," puts on six productions a year from mid-June through early September.

Another staple of summer entertainment, the Cape Cod Melody Tent in Hyannis, got its start as the Cape Cod Music Circus in 1950 during a time when tent theaters were found in resort areas around the country. Richard Aldrich, director of the Cape Playhouse, and

The Theatre Workshop of Nantucket, located at Bennett Hall in downtown Nantucket, has been staging plays on the island since 1956. It offers a season of seven productions from June through December.

The Cape Playhouse and the Melody Tent are two entertainment venues with long, colorful pasts. Below photo by Paul Scharff

his wife, actress Gertrude Lawrence, spearheaded the venture, staging summer seasons of operettas and Broadway-style musicals. Today, after ownership changes and renovations that included replacing the canvas tent with a state-of-the art vinyl one adorned with a cupola, the Melody Tent is a popular 2,300-seat concert venue featuring top headliners.

There are now an estimated three dozen theater companies staging live productions in communities across the Cape and the islands. Each one is part of what makes the region much more than the usual sand-and-surf destination.

VINTAGE VENUES

WHAT: Cape Playhouse, Cape Cod Melody Tent

WHERE: 820 Main St., Dennis; 41 W Main St., Hyannis

COST: Varies

PRO TIP: Want to learn more? *A History of Theater on Cape Cod* (History Press) by Sue Mellen is an invaluable resource.

A LITTLE NIGHT MUSIC

Who is the Phantom Organist?

While many of the 18th- and 19th-century homes lining Yarmouth Port's Old King's Highway are steeped in ghost stories, the goings-on at number 361 veer from the typical footsteps and door slamming. Here's the story.

In 1969, four months after moving into the antique Greek Revival, Pat Anderson, a nurse at Cape Cod Hospital, and her husband, Don, settled into the front bedroom. As Don drifted off, Pat began to hear the faint sound of organ music, which gradually grew louder until she could recognize the hymn as Bach's "Jesu, Joy of Man's Desiring."

Like the soundtrack to a haunted house, ominous music played most nights, at times so loud that Pat would get up and take her book to the kitchen. The phantom organist sometimes took a break for a few nights and then started up again.

Don never heard the music and suggested that someone might be playing an organ across the street. "It's coming from the bedroom," Pat told him. "I know I'm not imagining this." She delved into the history of the 19th-century house, finding that the master bedroom had once been a parlor.

Adding to the mystery, the cellar door in the front room would fling open between Thanksgiving and Christmas, year after year. It always happened when the family was out of the room, and anything placed on top of the door—no matter how heavy—would be flung aside.

THE CHAPTER HOUSE INN

WHAT: Victorian mansion turned inn, built in 1716 (and a nearby haunted house)

WHERE: 277 Rte. 6A, Yarmouth Port

COST: Varies by season

PRO TIP: Stop by the Chapter House Inn for a drink—the patio is open to the public.

After an extensive renovation, this 300-year-old mansion opened in 2022 as the Chapter House Inn. Photo courtesy of the Chapter House Inn

One afternoon, while chatting with the secretary at her son's school, Pat finally discovered that others had heard the organ as well. "Oh, you live in the old Baker house!" the secretary said. "Doesn't the music drive you crazy?" As it turns out, the organ music can only be heard by women.

With a history stretching back 300 years, the nearby Chapter House Inn is a hot spot for ghost stories. Guests have reported a rocking chair that turns during the night to face a blank wall (that once held a window), among other happenings.

GOREY'S HAUNT

Who was this master of gothic horror in a full-length fur coat?

There's a rack of fur coats in the kitchen and a doll thrown headfirst down the staircase at this 200-year-old sea captain's house. Renowned artist and author Edward Gorey (1925–2000) bought the Yarmouth Port house in 1979—attracted to its unkempt yard and air of decay—filling it with 25,000 books and 21 furs. It's now a museum celebrating his work and life.

Even if you've never heard of Gorey, you'll probably recognize his fanciful, eerie illustrations of Victorian and Edwardian characters. You might have seen his iconic animated opening sequence for the PBS *Mystery!* series. (The fallen doll is a reference to *The Gashlycrumb Tinies*, a story of 26 hapless children in alphabetical order: "A is for Amy who fell down the stairs; B is for Basil assaulted by bears ....")

A child prodigy from Chicago, Gorey was reading Agatha Christie mysteries and Bram Stoker's *Dracula* by age 5 and Victor Hugo by 8. He studied French literature at Harvard, taking weekend trips to the Cape to visit cousins.

By the 1970s he was famous, earning millions as the set and costume designer for the 1977 Broadway revival of *Dracula* and winning a Tony Award for costume design. Gorey's own costume in Manhattan was a fur coat plus "eight or nine pounds of jewelry" over jeans and ratty white tennis shoes, said Gregory Hischak, the museum's director. (An ardent animal lover, Gorey gave up the furs in 1985.)

He was addicted to the work of New York City Ballet choreographer George Balanchine, attending 9,000 performances and saving every ticket stub. After Balanchine died, in the mid-1980s, Gorey packed up his Manhattan studio apartment—leaving

While Gorey's books were usually considered too dark for children, he influenced the children's book authors Maurice Sendak, Shel Silverstein, and Lemony Snicket.

THE EDWARD GOREY HOUSE

WHAT: House museum celebrating the life and work of Edward Gorey

WHERE: 8 Strawberry Ln., Yarmouth Port

COST: $10, $8 seniors, students, and teachers

PRO TIP: Yarmouth Port's Jack's Outback was Gorey's go-to breakfast and lunch spot.

Top: *Edward Gorey bought this house with his earnings from the 1977 Broadway revival of* Dracula. *Photo by Paul Scharff.* Inset: *Museumgoers search for the 26 children who've met untimely ends in the Gashlycrumb Tinies Scavenger Hunt, beginning with "A is for Amy who fell down the stairs." Photo by Linda Humphrey*

a mummy's head in the closet—and took off for the weathered Cape house. His book *The Deranged Cousins, Or Whatever*, set on Cape Cod, has the three cousins meeting absurd ends, the last carried off by an unusually high tide.

ON LOCATION

Where can you pick up a paperback book at 2 a.m.?

This storied 19th-century bookshop starred in *The Storied Life of A.J. Fikry*, a 2022 movie based on Gabrielle Zevin's bestselling novel of the same name. It's also known for its sweet outdoor book stall, where you can pick up a book 24/7, paying by the honor system.

Step inside Parnassus Book Service and you'll find everything from beach reads to vintage posters to rare books. The three-story Victorian house with sloping floors opened as the Knowles General Store in 1840 and has housed the family-run bookstore since 1960.

For its role as Island Books, set on the fictional Alice Island off Cape Cod, the film crew turned the bookshop's light-blue trim purple and flanked its doorway with pink hydrangeas. A utility pole and power lines in front of the house were digitally erased.

The real-life bookshop was founded by Ben and Ruth Muse, who met at Columbia University and launched a mail-order book service in New York City before

PARNASSUS BOOK SERVICE

WHAT: Historic bookstore and movie location

WHERE: 220 Cranberry Hwy. (Rte. 6A), Yarmouth Port

COST: Varies. Free to browse. Signed first-edition Gorey books range from $95 to $350.

PRO TIP: Discover 22 fabulous indie bookstores on the Cape and islands at capeandislands-bookstoretrail.com. Titcomb's Bookshop in Sandwich, for one, is known for its many author events.

The Lighthouse Inn's waterfront restaurant in West Dennis also appeared in the *Fikry* movie, serving as Pequod's restaurant and a wedding venue.

A sign asks after-hours book hounds to leave their money in the mail slot on the front door. Photo by Linda Humphrey

moving to the Cape. Two of their eight children now run the nostalgic shop, and every book is available to order online.

You'll also find Edward Gorey's signed first editions here. The six-foot-two illustrator and writer, a Muse family friend, was often found sprawled on the shop's wooden floor, surrounded by books.

THE UNINVITED

Is this old-world restaurant haunted by a dentist and his mistress?

You won't have the chance to spend the night at the oldest inn on the Cape, which may be a good thing. The Old Yarmouth Inn is strictly a restaurant and tavern now, but you just might catch sight of its resident ghost while digging into a plate of shrimp scampi by the fireplace. One Thanksgiving, co-owner Sheila FitzGerald saw the ghost of Bradford Powell walk right by the host stand.

Scores of people, in fact, have reported seeing Powell—an apparition with a fluffy crown of white hair and jowls—at this former stagecoach stop that dates back to 1696. Guests have woken during the night to see his ghost glaring at them.

Powell owned the house in the late 19th and early 20th centuries, setting up his dental practice on the first floor. His family lived upstairs among rooms rented to teachers, one of whom happened to be Powell's mistress. Her spirit is said to roam the upstairs halls, meddling with guests in the night.

A friend visiting FitzGerald and her husband, Arpad Voros, who have owned the inn since 1996, packed up to leave after just one night. On the porch with his suitcase, he told the couple that he had felt someone sit on the bed while he was sleeping. He opened

OLD YARMOUTH INN

WHAT: Stagecoach stop and inn dating to 1696 turned old-world restaurant

WHERE: 223 Rte. 6A, Yarmouth Port

COST: Varies

PRO TIP: The three-course "Pre-6" menu, served from 4–6 p.m., is $34–$44.

The restaurant keeps a guest registry from the 1860s in the lobby.

his eyes, but no one was there. The ghost then tickled his feet and shook the bedposts, slamming the bed onto the floor over and over. Just as he finished this story, Voros's 93-year-old mother showed up, complaining about all the banging she had heard during the night.

Step into the 17th century at this stagecoach stop turned cozy restaurant. Photo by Linda Humphrey

WHO STOLE THE PORTRAIT OF CAPTAIN HALLET?

What's the story behind the art heist at this sea-captain's house museum?

Set along a stretch of pristine 19th-century homes, the Captain Bangs Hallet House Museum was once the unlikely scene of an art heist, a still-unsolved crime that shocked the town of Yarmouth Port.

In 1988, two thieves grabbed the caretaker of this jewel-box museum and tied her to a chair. They then ran through the Greek Revival house, snatching six 19th-century paintings, a rare 13th-century Chinese plate, a 200-piece scrimshaw collection, and several vases.

They took the portraits of Captain Hallet and his daughter but left the painting of his wife, Anna, which led investigators to speculate that they were working from a collector's shopping list.

The fully furnished house museum showcases portraits of several local sea captains, along with their stories, and model ships.

Anna Hallet's portrait is original, while Captain Hallet's portrait was re-created by Yarmouth artist Heather Braginton-Smith. Photos by Linda Humphrey

A sea captain in the China–India trade, Hallet and his family had their portraits painted at the port in Canton by a well-known Chinese artist, Lam Qua (also known as Kwan Kiu Cheong). His wife's portrait, as it turns out, was painted by an apprentice and is less valuable.

With the six missing paintings re-created by Yarmouth artist Heather Braginton-Smith, the house, built in 1840, is set up to depict the Hallet family's Victorian-era life.

A man believed to be one of the thieves had toured the historic-house museum the day before the heist, drawing attention by refusing to sign the guest book or pay the $1 donation. Even with this man's description, the culprits have not been caught and the items have not been recovered.

The heist is thought to be related to the 1990 theft at the Isabella Stewart Gardner Museum in Boston and is mentioned in the 2021 Netflix documentary *This Is a Robbery: the World's Biggest Art Heist.*

BROADWAY TO BOG

What prompted Annie Walker to abandon show business to run one of the Cape's last surviving cranberry farms?

In the midst of a successful career as a wardrobe supervisor for major Broadway productions, Annie Walker, suffering from burnout, left the bright lights behind in the 1990s to pursue the less glamorous life of a cranberry farmer. The 12th-generation Cape Codder headed straight back to her roots, purchasing a farm in Dennis that had once belonged to her grandfather. After a lot of hard work restoring the large cranberry bog out back, Annie's Crannies made its debut.

For just a few weekends a year during the cranberry harvest in October and November, Annie's Crannies draws a faithful audience of enthusiasts who stop by the farm's gift shop to purchase not only fresh berries but gift boxes that include honey and beeswax candles derived from the cranberry flower blossoms.

"It's showtime for a brief time—a limited run," says Walker in a video posted on her website (anniescrannies.com) in which she also comments on the increasing challenges of growing cranberries. "A barrel of berries commands only a third of what it did 25 years ago. Emotions and stupidity—that's what keeps me going."

Cranberries, one of just three species of fruit native to North America, have a long association with Cape Cod. For thousands of years before English settlement, the Wampanoag used wild cranberries not only for food but for dye and medicine. The first domestic cultivation of the tart-and-tangy fruit began around 1816, when a Dennis farmer, Revolutionary War veteran Captain Henry Hall, noticed that his wild cranberries grew better when sand was

---

The name *cranberry* is derived from "crane berry," so called because cranberry flowers resemble the heads of Sandhill cranes, birds that once frequented cranberry bogs.

Annie's Crannies is a vanishing example of a family-owned cranberry farm. Photo by Linda Humphrey

FRUITFUL HARVEST

WHAT: Annie's Crannies

WHERE: 36 Scarsdale Rd., Dennis

COST: Varies

PRO TIP: The Harwich Historical Society Museum at Brooks Academy in Harwich has a permanent *Cranberry Culture* exhibit devoted to cranberry history on Cape Cod.

blown over them. He started transplanting the vines and spreading sand on them, inspiring others to do the same.

By the early 1900s, cranberries were such a vital industry in southeastern Massachusetts that children were often excused from school to help with the harvest. Due to climate change, hybrid varieties, and mechanized harvesting methods, Massachusetts has been eclipsed as a cranberry producer by Wisconsin. A steady drop in wholesale prices and a decline in the cranberry juice industry has hurt the industry overall.

Despite this, Annie's Crannies is one of several cranberry enterprises still surviving on the Cape. Opportunities to witness the colorful harvest include Cranberry Bog Tours in Harwich, where Leo and Andrea Cakounes operate the largest organic cranberry bog on the Cape. Participants learn about the year-round management of a cranberry bog, see the equipment, and visit the farm animals.

SOLD!

Where can you get in the bidding fray at a New England country auction?

A classic white 19th-century sea captain's cottage off historic Route 6A in Dennis is an endangered species: a place to attend a live country auction. Country auctions, usually held in barns or on the grounds of farmhouses, were once a staple of American rural life, and one of the rare places to still get the feel of them is at Eldred's, the oldest auction house in New England.

Eldred's holds an average of 25 auctions per year, most of them online, but there are also several in-person sales during the summer where generations of bidders have gathered under the green-and-white striped tent by the barn to vie for items. The public can also stop by Eldred's during auction preview days to peruse the lots up for bid. Considered the world's premier auction house for maritime art, Eldred's also draws collectors worldwide for sales pertaining to Americana, Asian and European art, collectibles, fine art, historic documents, military items, and much more.

"I think people are often surprised that we offer the kind of high-quality valuable items that tend to be associated with the largest city auction houses," said Josh Eldred, who heads the auction house founded by his father, Robert, in 1947. "We routinely sell objects for more than $100,000, and we have even sold works of art for over a million dollars."

Eldred is quick to add that there are also treasures to be won at bargain prices. "One of the biggest surprises is that you can buy a

ON THE BLOCK

WHAT: Eldred's, New England's oldest auction house

WHERE: 1483 Rte. 6A, Dennis

COST: Depends on timing, tenacity, and luck

PRO TIP: If you can't attend a preview in person, the lots for upcoming auctions can be viewed on Eldred's website (eldreds.com)

Gathering in Eldred's green-and-white-striped auction tent has long been a summer tradition for collectors.

200-year-old antique bureau from us for less than one would cost at a place like Pottery Barn," he said.

Even if auctions have grown less personal over the years, Eldred thinks they retain a magic quality that makes them irresistible to collectors. "You can't just come into the gallery and buy an item; you have to go through the auction process," he said. "It's a bit like a gambler's rush—sometimes you get a great deal and buy it for less that you expect, sometimes you get caught up and spend more than you had planned!"

Believing that female artists are seriously undervalued by the art world, Eldred's recently launched "Women in the Arts" auctions solely devoted to paintings, sculpture, mixed media, photography, and other works created by women. Some of the proceeds from the sales go to WE CAN, a local women's empowerment organization.

INTO THE WOODS

What's the story behind this whimsical pottery village set in a pine grove?

Moorish palaces, Cinderella castles, and ceramic wind chimes hang from trees and top pedestals at this oh-so-enchanting pottery studio in the woods, established in 1952.

Founded by the late artist Harry Holl, Scargo Pottery & Art Gallery was modeled after a Japanese pottery village. Inspired by meeting the Japanese potter and Zen Buddhist Shoji Hamada and less enamored of the art-world scene, Holl centered his life around pottery.

Growing up in a rough neighborhood in the Bronx, Holl learned to draw and paint from a renter in his family's house. He trained at LaGuardia High School of Music & Art—the high school that inspired the *Fame* movies—and then moved on to Manhattan's Beaux-Arts Institute of Design and the Art Students League of New York before decamping to North Carolina's Black Mountain College.

At the legendary but short-lived liberal arts school near Asheville, Holl met his first wife,

SCARGO POTTERY & ART GALLERY

WHAT: Japanese-inspired pottery village and artisan shop

WHERE: 54 Studio Way, Dennis

COST: Varies. Free to explore the gallery

PRO TIP: Ensconced in a Civil War–era home, Scargo Cafe has a clubby, old-world aura. Plus, it's rumored to be haunted.

The fish-shaped bird feeders designed by Harry Holl in the 1950s are bestsellers.

A woodland wonderland filled with clay works of art. Photos by Linda Humphrey

Mirande. Her father, the sculptor Arnold Geissbuhler, had a summer studio above Scargo Lake in Dennis, where Holl soon joined the family. He co-founded the nearby Cape Cod Museum of Art in 1981, with a mission to display and preserve the works of Cape-based artists.

The couple had four daughters who grew up working with clay, often molding it into castles. All are artists, and two, Tina Holl and Kim Holl, own Scargo Pottery along with artist Meden Parker. The year-round studio has an open-door policy. . . . Stop by for holiday cheer on the first Sunday in December, when they give out 700 cups of eggnog.

BREWSTER'S WONDERLAND

Where will you find a cottage inside an opulent mansion?

Stepping through the Crosby Mansion's ornate parlor doorway, you'll find yourself, much like Alice in Wonderland, inside a curiously smaller house. This four-room cottage continues the storybook theme as you stroll through the keeping room, passing a doorway that leads to nowhere.

Reluctant to tear down his boyhood home in Brewster, Albert Crosby wrapped the 1888 mansion around his 1832 homestead. The mystery doorway, which ends at a wall, once led to several more rooms of the cottage, which were razed to make way for the three-story, 35-room Romanesque manor.

Crosby left Brewster at age 25 for Chicago, where he sold alcohol to the US Army during the Civil War. He returned home at 49 with a fortune and a 28-year-old onetime showgirl, Matilda, his new bride.

The couple designed their 18,000-square-foot estate with a foyer inspired by Buckingham Palace, a parlor inspired by Versailles, and a billiards room inspired by an Adirondack hunting lodge.

By the late 1930s, the mansion had been sold to the Cape Cod Institute of Music, which gave way to an inn and restaurant in the '50s and then to a diet camp for girls in the '70s. Abandoned and boarded up in the '80s, the once-dazzling mansion was set to be demolished for a parking lot. Vandals broke in, setting fires.

THE CROSBY MANSION

WHAT: Gilded Age mansion

WHERE: 163 Crosby Ln., Brewster

COST: $5 donation. Docent-led tours offered on Wednesdays and Sundays

PRO TIP: Don't miss the view of Cape Cod Bay from the balcony on the third floor, once the servants' quarters.

Returning from Chicago with a fortune and a showgirl, Albert Crosby built a palatial summer house around his rustic boyhood home. Photos by Linda Humphrey

A group of volunteers finally restored the estate in the '90s, its hand-carved mahogany and oak moldings and 13 unique tiled fireplaces intact. It's easy to picture the Gilded Age manor's heyday, when guests included Mark Twain and the Duke of Wales. Amid all the glitzy parties, Albert still took comfort in his boyhood cottage, retreating there when he needed a break.

The extra-wide foyer door was designed to accommodate hoop skirts.

FARM TO TABLES

Where will you find a farm-to-table garden party?

Just about everyone knows that the Chatham Bars Inn is a dream of a hotel. This fabled seaside resort, known as CBI, is teeming with luxuries, the latest of which involves digging into heirloom tomato bruschetta and bramble berries with lemon verbena on a farm—and you won't have to be a hotel guest to join in.

With a touch of CBI glamour, the resort's farm in Brewster serves weekly alfresco dinners under strings of lights, beginning with signature welcome cocktails. Chefs craft four-course spreads—which include locally sourced seafood and meats along with just-picked fare—from June to November, with fall dinners moving into the heated greenhouse.

As we toured the eight-acre farm, Assistant Farm Manager Kevin Nadeau handed out treats in the form of just-picked cherry tomatoes while pointing out endless rows of flawless produce—over 30 varieties of tomatoes, over 20 varieties of peppers—all planted and harvested by hand.

Back at the resort, chefs at five restaurants—from the fine-

CBI FARM

WHAT: Alfresco farm-to-table dinners

WHERE: 3034 Main St., Brewster

COST: Farm-to-table dinners are $150–$200 per person, including your choice of red or white wine, welcome cocktail, tax, and gratuity.

PRO TIP: The Wednesday dinner will be held on Thursday in case of rain, so keep the night after your dinner reservation open.

Besides CBI, the farm partners with several other farm-to-table restaurants, including Sunbird in Orleans, the Brewster Fish House, and the buzzy Pheasant in Dennis, which is owned by a young couple from NYC.

Top: *Chatham Bars Inn brings the table to the farm.* Photo courtesy of Cape Cod Chamber of Commerce. Inset: *Assistant Farm Manager Kevin Nadeau, along with a team of 30, grows 125 varieties of produce and flowers.* Photo by Linda Humphrey

dining Stars to the Beach House Grill—plan their menus along with the farm managers, and private clambakes—also available to nonguests—add corn and potatoes from the farm.

You can also pick up your own vegetables and flowers, along with PB Boulangerie bread and other local provisions, at the farm stand. It's worth a visit just to marvel at the pristine, bright-green rows of produce. As the *Boston Globe* put it, "both its beauty and its CBI-ness will stun you."

LODGING AND SPIRITS

What brought the *Ghost Hunters* TV team to the Orleans Waterfront Inn?

When the Maas family bought this Victorian inn, a haunted mansion straight out of central casting, they hadn't heard the ghost stories. Once the scene of a murder, the manor built by a sea captain in 1875 had given way to a brothel and speakeasy run by the Irish mafia in the 1920s. As the story goes, a prostitute was stabbed by a customer at the front entrance.

By 1996, when Ed and Laurie Maas stepped in, the crumbling mansion had been abandoned. They had planned to tear it down until Laurie sensed a ghost as a sudden blast of cold air and convinced the family to save the manor.

As renovations began, Ed bought new locks and bolted the two front doors, returning the next morning to find them flung open. The ghost, thought to be the ill-fated prostitute, soon claimed Room 5. Two female guests, on two separate occasions, have refused to leave Room 5 for months, until their families were called in to take them home.

> ## ORLEANS WATERFRONT INN
>
> **WHAT:** 1875 mansion turned inn with a ghostly past
>
> **WHERE:** 3 Old County Rd., Orleans
>
> **COST:** Varies
>
> **PRO TIP:** Watch the *Ghost Hunters* episode (Season 6, Episode 8) on ghostsofnewengland.com

There's a secret storage space built into the lobby wall where the Irish mafia hid rum and cash.

Not ready to check in? The inn's waterfront deck is a fun spot for (non-spooky) dining. Photo courtesy of Orleans Historical Society

The inn is also rumored to be visited by the ghosts of Fred the bartender, who either hanged himself or was hanged in the cupola in the 1950s, and Paul the dishwasher, who hanged himself in the basement in the 1970s. There's even a ghost cat.

A team from the *Ghost Hunters* TV show showed up in 2010. Among other paranormal happenings, they heard a scream outside Room 5, communicated with the ghost prostitute by asking her to tap a flashlight, saw a shadow pass behind the cameraman in the lobby, heard muffled voices in the dining room, and recorded a voice in the cupola that sounded like "Let me out" or "Get me down."

THIS RESCUE INSPIRED A DISNEY MOVIE

Why are visitors obsessed with this small wooden boat at Rock Harbor?

Fans snap photos and climb aboard the wooden lifeboat docked at Rock Harbor in Orleans. They ask the docent about *The Finest Hours*, the 2016 Disney movie starring Chris Pine.

Hollywood picked up the *Finest Hours* story from the 2009 book of the same name, sparking renewed interest in what's been called the most daring small-boat rescue in Coast Guard history. Indeed, this lifeboat—and its legendary story—had been forgotten until 1981, when a photographer found it rotting in a field. Now fully restored, the lifeboat is the only operating survivor of its kind on the East Coast.

The movie may have altered the timeline of Bernie Webber's courtship—he and Miriam were already married at the time—but the storyline is true. On February 18, 1952, a nor'easter snowstorm of hurricane-force winds and 60-foot-

CG 36500 LIFEBOAT

WHAT: The most daring small-boat rescue in Coast Guard history

WHERE: Rock Harbor, 46 Anchor Dr., near Bay View Dr., Orleans

COST: Free to tour the boat with a docent

PRO TIP: The iconic Chatham Lighthouse, overlooking the infamous Chatham Bar, is one of the few lighthouses in America that still operates 24 hours a day. It's open for tours in the summer.

Fans will find *Finest Hours* exhibits at the Coast Guard Heritage Museum in Barnstable, housed in the exquisite Old Customs House, an Italian Renaissance Revival built in 1856.

Hop aboard the historic lifeboat that inspired a book and a Disney movie.
Photo by Linda Humphrey

high waves whipped across New England, splitting the SS *Pendleton* oil tanker in half. As night fell, the Chatham Coast Guard sent 23-year-old Webber and three volunteers out on the 12-person motor lifeboat known as CG 36500.

As waves shattered the boat's windshield and knocked out the compass, Webber somehow managed to find the sinking tanker by following the sound of twisting metal. With 32 stranded, freezing crewmen squeezed onboard, Webber navigated the lifeboat back to a cheering crowd at the Chatham Fish Pier.

GOING QUACKERS

Where can you find a rubber duckie suitable for any occasion?

Chatham, frequently hailed as one of the Cape's most charming beach towns, has something tucked along its main street that none of the others can claim: the world's largest rubber duck shop.

At Ducks in the Window, the shelves are filled with duckies of various sizes designed to match every occupation or interest. How about a fireman duck, sailor duck, golfer duck, lawyer duck, or teacher duck? Looking for a favorite celebrity, athlete, historic figure, or superhero? There are ducks depicting Batman, Darth Vader, Mick Jagger, Bruce Springsteen, Rocky Balboa, Queen Elizabeth II, Albert Einstein, Jane Austen, Shakespeare, and many, many others. Other ducks are outfitted properly for a college graduation, birthday, wedding, or other special occasion. The sizes vary too, ranging from miniature on up to jumbo.

Want something other than a rubber duck? There are plenty of other duck-themed items, including mugs, hats, and various accessories.

Owners Rob Foster and Colleen Cummings, a husband and wife who bought the shop a few years ago after Cummings got a part-time job there, estimate their duck selection represents over 1,000 subjects and styles. The couple has steadily expanded the enterprise to include an online business and wholesale operation that imports ducks from manufacturers around the world. They also established DITW Designs, which creates their own duck personas, starting with Teacher Duck in 2018.

Foster and Cummings say they are surprised at how quickly their rubber duckie empire has evolved and how busy it keeps them.

Among the best-selling rubber ducks are those depicting unicorns and Donald Trump.

DUCKS IN THE WINDOW

WHAT: World's largest store devoted to rubber duckies

WHERE: 507 Main St., Chatham

COST: $6.99 and up

PRO TIP: Don't see what you're looking for? You can order a rubber duck that is personalized just for you.

How much is that duckie in the window? Top photo courtesy of Massachusetts Office of Travel & Tourism. Inset photo by Maria Lenhart

"We have become a very, very, very unique seaside tourist shop that has grown to a national appeal," Cummings said. "It's exciting and scary."

ESCAPE ROOMS

What part did Cape Cod play in the Underground Railroad?

Secret passageways and trap doors leading to hidden cellars are found in old houses all over Cape Cod, evidence that the region played a significant if little-known role in the Underground Railroad, the network of safe havens that helped enslaved people make the perilous journey northward out of bondage. While the Underground Railroad is more closely associated with overland travel up through Ohio, some escapees made their way on maritime vessels heading from ports in the Carolinas along sea routes to New England, from where they could continue on to Canada. In many cases, enslaved dockworkers were able to pay sea captains to ferry them to freedom aboard their ships.

While no one knows how many slaves might have traveled through Cape Cod or the islands on their way north, properties associated with hiding escapees have been identified in Barnstable Village, West Barnstable, East Sandwich, Falmouth, Harwich, South Orleans, Provincetown, and Nantucket. Many were assisted by Quakers and other religious groups with strong abolitionist views.

Provincetown is believed to have four houses that served as way stations that offered food and shelter to runaways. One of these is at 54 Commercial St., a classic Cape Cod–style house built by Captain Stephen Nickerson that is one of the oldest surviving structures in town. Now a private residence, until a few years ago it was operated as a bed-and-breakfast inn called the 1807 House. A cluster of historic properties along the Old King's Highway (Route

Some of the white chimneys with black bands found on old Cape Cod houses are thought to have been a signal that the homes belonged to abolitionists who would shelter slaves traveling on the Underground Railroad.

It's not unusual to find hiding places for runaway slaves in old Cape Cod houses like Ashley Manor in Barnstable.

6A) are also associated with the Underground Railroad, including Ashley Manor, a former inn where a secret passage connects the lower and upper floors.

6A) are also associated with the Underground Railroad, including Ashley Manor, a former inn where a secret passage connects the lower and upper floors.

At least three inns on the Cape have connections with the Underground Railroad, including A Little Inn on Pleasant Bay in Orleans where a trapdoor in the inn's foyer leads to a small stone cellar thought to be a hiding place.

SAFE HAVENS

WHAT: A Little Inn on Pleasant Bay; The Tern Inn and Cottages

WHERE: 654 S Orleans Rd., Orleans; 91 Chase St., West Harwich

COST: Varies

PRO TIP: The book *Sailing to Freedom: Maritime Dimensions of the Underground Railroad* provides more insight on Cape Cod's relationship with the Underground Railroad.

The Tern Inn and Cottages in West Harwich also has a small trapdoor, this one in the living room floor leading to a round cellar where runaways could await ships leaving for Canada. At the Old Yarmouth Inn in Yarmouth, a hidden door in the attic leads to a secret room that is likely to have sheltered people in hiding.

TRAINING DAYS

Where have train enthusiasts preserved a vanished bit of railroad history?

The Chatham Railroad Museum is a sweet reminder of how important trains once were to small-town life. Founded in 1886, the Chatham Railroad once carried mail, cranberries, fresh fish, lumber, and thousands of passengers per year along a seven-mile spur that connected the little Cape town of Chatham with Harwich and, through connecting service, to New York City and beyond. At its height, the railroad operated four passenger trains a day and a freight train when needed, serving the needs of local residents as well as the increasing number of Cape Cod visitors. The railroad ceased operation in 1937, and the tracks were sold to Japan shortly thereafter.

"Highways and trucks put the trains out of business," said Jeff Gordon, a docent who greets visitors to the Chatham Railroad Museum. The museum is located in the original depot, a charming example of "Railroad Gothic" architecture with its wooden turrets and gingerbread

CHATHAM RAILROAD MUSEUM

WHAT: A museum dedicated to railroad history

WHERE: 153 Depot Rd., Chatham

COST: Free, but donations are encouraged

PRO TIP: Visit the nearby Chatham Marconi Maritime Center, which includes the Marconi/RCA-Wireless Museum with interactive exhibits on early wireless communications history.

Train enthusiasts from around the world have donated artifacts to the Chatham Railroad Museum. Photos by Linda Humphrey

trim that is on the National Register of Historic Places. Inside, the museum is packed with items donated by train enthusiasts from around the world, including lanterns, brass locomotive bells, menus, timetables, original paintings, a vintage vending machine, and assorted model trains.

A sign above the stationmaster's office advertises Western Union telegram service, while another sign asks visitors to refrain from combing their hair while in the depot.

"Western Union was a vital service for people in those days—people heavily relied on telegrams for communication," Gordon said, adding that the other sign was necessary because "lice was often a problem back then."

In back of the museum is a 1910 caboose from the New York Central Railroad that visitors can climb aboard and walk through. Used by train crews as a place to rest and relax between shifts, the caboose is equipped with bunks for napping and a small woodstove for preparing coffee or a light meal.

Model train enthusiasts head to Orleans to marvel at 2,000 square feet of train layouts in both rural and urban scenes. The Nauset Model Railroad Club (nausetmodelrrclub.com), located at 180 Route 6A, is free and open to visitors on Wednesday nights in July and August.

SEA CHANGE

Where can you learn about the Cape's seals and sharks, and where are the best spots to watch those adorable seals?

Once you've checked whale watching off your list, take a spin along Monomoy Island on a seal-watching cruise. Accessible only by boat, these uninhabited barrier beaches stretching eight miles south of Chatham host the largest gray seal colony on the East Coast.

Once rare in this area, seals began to establish pupping colonies on Monomoy in the 1990s. Their numbers have now surged into the tens of thousands—and they've brought the sharks back with them.

While seals and sharks have thrived off the coast here for thousands of years—Henry David Thoreau wrote about "tough stories of sharks all over the Cape" in 1865—Massachusetts put bounties on seals from 1888 to 1962. Amid fears that they were gobbling up too many fish, seal noses earned $5 each.

Ten years later, the federal Marine Mammal Protection Act banned seal hunting, and the seals eventually reclaimed their old turf. You'll spot gray seals, which have a horselike head, in summer (their genus/species name, *Halichoerus grypus*, means "hooked-nosed sea pig"), and harbor seals, which have puppylike faces, in colder months.

On the mainland, the Chatham Fish Pier observation deck is a sure bet for seal watching. Pick up a lobster roll and watch the fishermen offload the day's catch, throwing scraps to the seals. Or

---

Monomoy Island Excursions' 90-minute seal-watching tour glides through two harbors best viewed by boat: Harwich Port's Wychmere Harbor and Chatham's Stage Harbor. You'll get a waterfront view of the deactivated Stage Harbor Lighthouse, which is now a family's summer home.

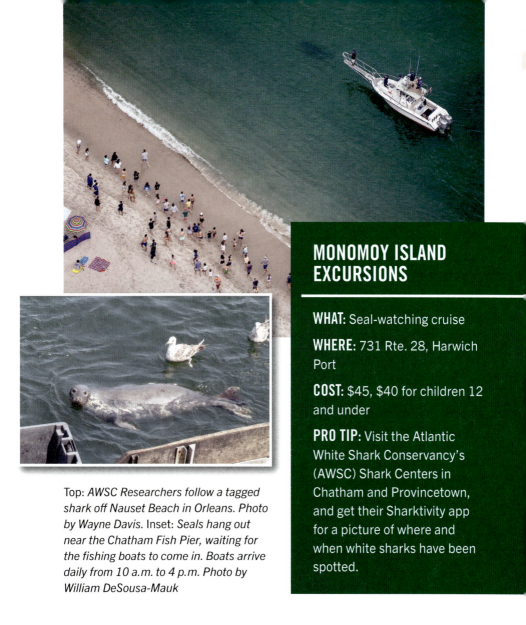

MONOMOY ISLAND EXCURSIONS

WHAT: Seal-watching cruise

WHERE: 731 Rte. 28, Harwich Port

COST: $45, $40 for children 12 and under

PRO TIP: Visit the Atlantic White Shark Conservancy's (AWSC) Shark Centers in Chatham and Provincetown, and get their Sharktivity app for a picture of where and when white sharks have been spotted.

Top: *AWSC Researchers follow a tagged shark off Nauset Beach in Orleans. Photo by Wayne Davis.* Inset: *Seals hang out near the Chatham Fish Pier, waiting for the fishing boats to come in. Boats arrive daily from 10 a.m. to 4 p.m. Photo by William DeSousa-Mauk*

stroll along Coast Guard Beach to see seals bobbing in the waves—most are about a mile down the shore, to the right of the parking lot. Just don't swim near them, as white sharks have been known to hunt for seals in shallow water. Despite those fear-inducing scenes in *Jaws*, you're not likely to see a shark's dorsal fin slice through the surface, said National Park Service Ranger Taryn Withers. White sharks typically hug the bottom of the ocean, Withers said, hunting by picking up electrical currents in salt water.

SCREEN GEMS, PART ONE

Is it a church, a drugstore, or a movie theater?

Few places are as endangered as historic movie palaces, but several treasures from the silver-screen era are thriving on Cape Cod, Martha's Vineyard, and Nantucket. In some cases, it took herculean efforts and a whole of ingenuity from the local community to keep them from disappearing into a celluloid oblivion.

Among them is the Chatham Orpheum Theater, which opened on the Main Street of Chatham back in 1916. First called the Orpheum Theater, it was renamed the Chatham Theater after its purchase by Interstate Theaters in the 1930s. The 300-seat theater served as the town's primary movie house until 1987, when it ceased operation and was subsequently converted to a CVS drugstore. While the interior was gutted for its new purpose, the theater's classic New England colonial-style exterior was spared.

When the CVS closed in 2011, local citizens launched a drive to "bring back movies to Main Street," and formed a group to raise funds to reopen the theater under its original Orpheum name. Within six months, $1.5 million in direct donations were raised, and a community grant was secured. The theater reopened in 2013 with two screening rooms showing current and classic films. A new lobby includes a pizza café and bar adorned with a vibrant mural called *The After Party* with depictions of iconic movie stars.

Another splendid survivor from the silver-screen era is the Cape Cinema in Dennis. While its exterior looks so much like a stately

Old movie houses like the Cape Cinema and Chatham Orpheum have a treasured place in Cape Cod communities.

New England church that it's logical to assume it once was a house of worship, the Cape Cinema, opened in 1930, has always been a movie house. Its art deco interior is a dazzling contrast to its vast ceiling mural depicting heavenly constellations and its original stage curtain adorned with a giant sunburst. The theater presents art-house films, simulcasts of the Metropolitan Opera, and occasional live music performances.

The Cape Cinema's biggest historical milestone occurred on August 11, 1939, when it presented the very first public screening of *The Wizard of Oz*. How did this unlikely premiere come to be? It happened because Margaret Hamilton, who played the Wicked Witch of the West, was performing that summer at the nearby Cape Playhouse and arranged for the screening to take place at the theater. Every year on August 11, the Cape Cinema screens *The Wizard of Oz* in 35 mm to commemorate the historic event.

Back in its pre-CVS era, the Chatham Theater was open only from spring until early fall and showed only evening performances, not matinees. The exception was during inclement weather, when it would open for "rainy day matinees" in recognition that people needed somewhere to go instead of the beach.

TWENTY-TWO YEARS AT SEA

Who built the ornate Second Empire–style manor in rural Eastham?

The Second Empire style, with its signature mansard roof, was all the rage in Paris in the mid-1800s. Most of rural Eastham, meanwhile, was dotted with homespun shingled cottages when sea captain Edward Penniman built his French Second Empire trophy house in 1868. Painted in bright Victorian-era colors with a gate fashioned from a 13-foot-tall whale's jawbone, the manor was a sight from the technicolor Land of Oz.

Whaling Captain Penniman returned to Fort Hill with a staggering fortune. Photo by Linda Humphrey

Edward Penniman (1831–1913) grew up in the Fort Hill section of Eastham and eventually married the girl who grew up across the street, Betsy Augusta Knowles. He called her Gustie. At 21, he set out on the first of his seven whaling expeditions as a boatsteerer, charged with the grisly task of harpooning the whale and hanging on as it dragged the whaleboat in what was known as a Nantucket Sleigh Ride. By 29, he was a captain.

Most of the whales in the Northeast had been killed by the mid-1800s, so New Bedford whale hunters were forced to sail to such faraway places as Hawaii, New Zealand, and the Arctic. As each expedition lasted about three years, Penniman spent 22 years at sea, with Gustie and two of their three children joining him for nine years.

CAPTAIN PENNIMAN HOUSE

WHAT: Sea captain's trophy home built in 1868

WHERE: 70 Fort Hill Rd., Eastham

COST: Free tours with the National Park Service

PRO TIP: Grab a bite at the nearby Arnold's Lobster & Clam Bar. Modeled after Arnold's 1950s malt shop from the TV show *Happy Days*, this seafood shack is no tourist trap.

The mansion stayed in the Penniman family until 1963, when the National Park Service bought it as part of the Cape Cod National Seashore. Now a museum, the house showcases several rooms of original furniture along with wallpaper from France and carpet from the Orient. The National Park Service declined to purchase all of the Penniman furniture because, well, as Ranger Brent Ellis put it, "we were just stupid."

Note the purely decorative marble-fireplace mantel. Wood-burning fireplaces were considered passé at the time, and firewood was scant, as all the trees on the Cape had been cut down.

NIGHT LIGHTS

Can someone else please set up the bonfire?

An hour before sunset, we kicked off our sandals and strolled Nauset Light Beach, passing a few crackling bonfires at the edge of the waves. Kids toasted marshmallows on sticks, their sand toys strewn about as their parents grabbed drinks from the cooler. A few seals popped their heads out of the water near the fishing poles, hoping to steal the catch.

This classic summer pastime won't cost you a cent, and the National Seashore's park rangers will even set up the bonfire for you. (Okay, technically, it's a campfire.)

With a retro summer-camp vibe, our group gathered around the fire as the two park rangers launched a game of *Jeopardy!*-like trivia. (The categories were Wildlife, Lighthouses, History & Culture, Geology, and Ships & Sailing, and we didn't know any of the answers.) These weekly ranger-led bonfires sometimes include storytelling and songs; in midsummer, they'll draw up to 100 beachgoers.

BEACH BONFIRES

WHAT: Campfires at Nauset Light Beach and other National Seashore beaches

WHERE: 105 Nauset Light Beach Rd., Eastham

COST: Free after 5 p.m., but you'll need a permit for the campfire

PRO TIP: If you're carrying your own firewood and beach-campfire gear, the easiest beaches to access are Coast Guard in Eastham and Herring Cove in Provincetown.

The weekly bonfire is just one of many free ranger-led events at the Cape Cod National Seashore. Stop by the Salt Pond or Province Lands Visitor Centers to pick up a flyer, or check their website at nps.gov/caco. Some programs require registration.

Families gather on Nauset Light Beach for twilight s'mores. Photo by Linda Humphrey

If you're up for building your own beach campfire, you'll need a free permit. Six National Seashore beaches allow fires, with each beach granting just four nightly permits. In July and August, show up at one of the visitor centers in person, three days in advance, when they open at 9 a.m.

For campfires at Coast Guard, Nauset Light, and Marconi Beaches, reserve a permit at Salt Pond Visitor Center in Eastham. For Head of the Meadow, Race Point, and Herring Cove beaches, reserve at Province Lands Visitor Center in Provincetown.

Whether you're joining the rangers or setting up your own get-together, don't forget insect repellent, sweatshirts, and beach chairs. And once the festivities end and the fire is doused with seawater, you'll need a flashlight to find your way back to the parking lot.

FAR FROM THE MADDING SUMMER CROWDS

Where will you find a beach not overrun by tourists (in July) and an iconic mid-century modern cottage?

With lines for ice cream winding around the block and traffic crawling on Route 6, is there any escape from the summer crush? Do secret beaches actually exist on the Cape?

Southern Living magazine lists Wellfleet's Bound Brook Island as one of the Best Secret Beaches in the US (#6), so we opted to try it on a jam-packed Fourth of July weekend, pulling into the Duck Harbor parking lot on a sunny, 80-degree Friday. A three-minute walk up a sand bluff brought us to the crashing waves of Cape Cod Bay, remote and wild. We saw just two beachgoers as we strolled along the surf: a woman lounging in a beach chair with a book and a guy walking two dogs.

After a 15-minute beach jaunt, we found the modernist Hatch Cottage perched on a bluff in the pine woods overlooking the bay. Built in 1962, the weathered beach house was designed by Jack Hall for Robert Hatch, an editor of the *Nation*, and Ruth Hatch, a painter.

Like many of Wellfleet's modern homes, the 784-square-foot cottage "is like a high-concept dune shack," designed for outdoor living, said Peter McMahon, founding executive director of the

---

Check the map and you'll notice that Bound Brook Island is no longer an island. In a misguided effort to combat mosquitoes, the town blocked the tidal flow of saltwater into the Herring River more than a century ago. Plans are now underway to restore the river.

Cape Cod Modern House Trust. With a matrix of three cubes connected by outdoor decks—one is the living room and kitchen, two are bedrooms—you'll have to step outside to move between rooms.

Self-taught architect Jack Hall, a blue-blooded Princeton grad who drove an old Rolls-Royce and married four times, arrived in Wellfleet in the late 1930s and moved there full-time in the '70s. For a time, he was known as the Squire of Bound Brook.

Stocked with the family's original furnishings, books, and paintings, the Hatch Cottage is available for rustic summer getaways (no internet, heat, laundry, or dishwasher). Photo by Antoine Lorgnier. Courtesy of the Cape Cod Modern House Trust

BOUND BROOK ISLAND

WHAT: Secret beach without crowds and an iconic mid-century modern cottage

WHERE: Bound Brook Island Rd., Wellfleet

COST: Free

PRO TIP: Visitors staying in Wellfleet can buy a beach-parking sticker at the town pier. Not staying in Wellfleet? Park at the Atwood-Higgins House on the right side of the road (free) and walk about a mile down Bound Brook Island Road to the sand dunes. For information on renting or touring the Hatch Cottage, contact capemoderntrust@gmail.com

OUTER CAPE PIONEERS

How did Wellfleet become an outpost of modernist architecture?

Back when New Yorkers could take the train from Grand Central Station to the Outer Cape, from the mid-1920s to the mid-1960s, a bohemian subculture took root in the towns of Wellfleet, Truro, and Provincetown. Land was cheap as three self-taught designer-builders from well-heeled families—Jack Phillips, Jack Hall, and Hayden Walling—arrived in the 1930s to build folk-modernist cottages in the Wellfleet woods, their avant-garde houses with flat roofs, boxlike shapes, and expansive windows soon filling with a flock of intellectuals and creative types.

Bostonian Jack Phillips (1908–2003), whose ancestors founded Phillips Exeter Academy and Phillips Academy Andover, inherited 800 acres of oceanside Wellfleet woodland in the late 1920s. After studying art at Harvard and in Paris, he set about building the Turkey Houses—six cabins built from turkey coops on Horseleech Pond—among other projects. (When Phillips died at age 94, he was buried with a roll of duct tape, said to be his favorite building material.)

Phillips sold pieces of land to friends, among them 18-year-old Walling and the European modernist architects who began to arrive in the 1940s, including Bauhaus-school founder Walter

Left: *Inspired by Frank Lloyd Wright, Charles Zehnder designed the Kugel/Gips House, which hovers over Wellfleet's Northeast Pond.* Right: *A wooden sign nailed to a tree points the way to Marcel Breuer's house in the Wellfleet woods. Photos courtesy of the Cape Cod Modern House Trust*

Gropius, Serge Chermayeff, Marcel Breuer, and structural engineer Paul Weidlinger.

About 95 modernist cottages are still scattered through the Wellfleet woods, including four managed by the Cape Cod Modern House Trust offering tours, summer rentals, and artist-in-residence programs: the 1953 Weidlinger House, the 1960 Kohlberg House, the 1962 Hatch House, and the 1970 Charles Zehnder–designed Kugel/Gips House.

The train proved convenient for the contentious marriage of Edmund Wilson and Mary McCarthy in the 1940s, when one or the other would storm out of their Wellfleet house after an argument, walk to the station, and catch the train back to New York.

JAM & BREAD

You know where to find the best oysters and chowder on the Cape, but do you know where to get the best jam and bread?

You'd probably drive right by this adorable roadside stand if you hadn't heard that it has quite a reputation. In-the-know vacationers have been picking up handmade jam from this rustic cottage along Route 6, summer after summer, since 1932.

Wellfleet's BriarLane Jams & Jellies—not to be confused with the equally wonderful Green Briar Jam Kitchen in Sandwich—has caught the attention of the *New York Times*, the *Boston Globe*, *Food & Wine*, and *Travel + Leisure*.

It all started during the Depression, when Esther Wiles set out jars of her homemade wild beach plum jelly on a card table in front of her home on Briar Lane. Her husband, Leroy, recently out of work, soon built the white-shingled roadside cottage, which he tended along with their collie, Tippy.

The Wiles family has been cooking up Esther's jam and jelly recipes ever since. With Terri Sayre, wife of Esther Wiles's grandson, now at the helm, BriarLane offers 45 varieties of jams, jellies, pickles, and chutneys. The hand-picked, hand-pressed beach-plum jelly is still a bestseller, Sayre said, along with blueberry, peach-raspberry, and strawberry.

This all-American beach town also happens to have a renowned French bakery, PB Boulangerie Bistro. French chef-owner Phillippe Rispoli arrived in Wellfleet with his American wife, who had spent her childhood summers there.

The clock at Wellfleet's First Congregational Church is the only town clock in the world that strikes on ship's time, according to Ripley's Believe It or Not!

BRIARLANE JAMS & JELLIES

WHAT: Iconic jam and jelly stand

WHERE: 3111 US-6, Wellfleet

COST: $6.95–$13.95

PRO TIP: The $13.95 Beach Plum Jelly is only available to those who know to ask for it—it's never on display.

Open since 1932, this little stand has attracted a flurry of press.
Photos by Linda Humphrey

Rispoli's French co-owner Boris Villatte (the B in PB) left Wellfleet in 2013 to open his own bakery, Falmouth's Maison Villatte, where the line often spills onto the sidewalk. *Food & Wine*'s writers are obsessed, ranking the boulangerie among the 100 best bakeries in America: "How a beach destination became such a patisserie magnet, sustaining at least three very good French bakeries that we know of, well, that's just so Cape Cod."

SOMEWHERE, BEYOND THE SEA, PART TWO

Where will you find the hidden ponds?

Buzzing with families and strewn with sand pails, Wellfleet's three big ponds—Great, Long, and Gull—require a coveted parking sticker. While the same clans tend to stake out these swimming spots summer after summer, anyone staying in town can pick up a sticker at the beach office.

The smaller kettle ponds, hidden in the Wellfleet woods, are trickier to find, with no signs to point the way. The Wellfleet Information Booth, unlike the locals, will equip you with a map and directions.

If you're up for traipsing through the backwoods to a far-flung pond, Dyer Pond, set in a pine forest, is a 15-minute walk from the Great Pond parking lot. You'll spot the dirt path, carpeted with pine needles, in the northwest corner of the lot. Go right at the fork, and as you catch a glimpse of the Dyer sign, follow the wooden steps to splash into the water.

Out-of-the-way Duck Pond, meanwhile, is best reached by a one-mile trek from the Wellfleet Hollow State Campground, while Higgins and Williams are best reached by paddling a kayak or canoe from Gull Pond.

From Higgins Pond, the mid-century modern Weidlinger House looks like a white box floating above the ground. (Book a tour or summer getaway with the Cape Cod Modern House Trust.)

WELLFLEET PONDS

WHAT: Kettle ponds hidden in the woods

WHERE: Start at the Wellfleet Information Booth, 1410 Rte. US-6

COST: $70 for a three-day parking sticker. Free after 5 p.m.

PRO TIP: Don't miss Wellfleet's summer hangouts: seafood eateries Mac's Shack and Moby Dick's, and the 1957 drive-in movie theater.

Clockwise from top left: *Gull Pond, Dyer Pond, walking to Dyer Pond, and Long Pond.*
Bottom two photos by Linda Humphrey

Beyond Wellfleet, you'll find hidden ponds along winding dirt roads, often with no signs. Try Goose Pond in Chatham, Hawkness Pond in Harwich, and Seymour Pond in Brewster's Punkhorn Parklands conservation area.

The Old Ladies Against Underwater Garbage are on a mission to pull trash out of the ponds. For more information: olaug-ma.com

HOPPER'S LIGHT FANTASTIC

How did Cape Cod landscapes inspire one of America's foremost artists?

While Edward Hopper is perhaps best known for *Nighthawks*, his seminal painting depicting urban loneliness, Cape Cod, evoking its own type of solitude in vast shorelines, scrub-covered dunes, and weathered buildings, also figured prominently in his work. It's not surprising given that Hopper spent nearly half of his 84 summers in Truro, most of them residing with his wife Josephine, also an artist, in a modest cottage with a huge picture window on a bluff overlooking a pristine beach on Cape Cod Bay.

The Hoppers lived a simple life in Truro when they purchased the secluded cottage surrounded by grasslands on Fisher Beach in 1934, reveling in the privacy and doing without a telephone, refrigerator, or electricity until 1951. "It's just a summer cottage as primitive as the land it's in," Josephine wrote to a friend.

Hopper was entranced by the light and the subtle colors emanating from the broad, empty expanses of sea and sky he saw on the Outer Cape. He soon found a wealth of subjects to paint in both watercolors and oils, resulting in such works as *Corn Hill*, a group of houses in sun and shadow atop the grassy dune where the *Mayflower* Pilgrims were said to have stolen a cache of corn from Native Americans in 1620.

Where can you see the Cape Cod sites depicted in Hopper's paintings? While some of the buildings have been demolished and many of the landscapes are no longer as they appeared in decades past, some are still to be found. Among them is the Highland

Rather than working in a studio, Hopper actually painted many of his Cape Cod subjects from the roadway while in his car.

Edward Hopper loved to paint local scenes during his 34 summers in North Truro.

Lighthouse (*Highland Light, North Truro*), which he painted in 1930. Although the lighthouse was moved back from the crumbling shoreline in 1996 by the National Park Service, which maintains the building and offers tours from mid-May to mid-October, it still resembles the painting. Other nearby buildings painted by Hopper include the Provincetown Library and an old house at Truro Vineyards.

As for Hopper's house on Fisher Beach, it's privately owned and not open to the public, but can still be viewed when walking along the shore. The house is not as isolated as it was when Hopper lived there, however. While local Truro residents waged a decade-long legal battle to remove a large, modern house near the Hopper cottage, claiming it was built illegally, they lost and the owners were finally allowed to occupy the house in 2019.

HIGHLAND LIGHT

WHAT: Historic lighthouse painted by Edward Hopper and open for public tours

WHERE: 27 Highland Light Rd., North Truro

COST: Adults $8, students $5

PRO TIP: The Highland House Museum, next door to the lighthouse and operated by the Truro Historical Society, has a permanent exhibit dedicated to Edward and Josephine Hopper and their life in Truro. The exhibit includes watercolors by Josephine as well as memorabilia and images of Edward Hopper paintings next to photographs of how the sites look today.

ODE TO A SWEDISH NIGHTINGALE

Why is there a tower in North Truro named for a 19th-century diva?

Rising in the midst of scrub oak thicket in an almost impenetrable spot on the Outer Cape is a 70-foot tower resembling a crenelated battlement from a fairy-tale castle. Called the Jenny Lind Tower, it's named for a Swedish singer who, back in her day, was a star on the magnitude of Taylor Swift. What in the world is a structure fit for Rapunzel doing in such an incongruous setting?

The story has its origins in a concert tour arranged for Lind, the so-called "Swedish Nightingale," by the impresario P. T. Barnum in 1850. Among the stops on the tour was a date to play in Boston at the Fitchburg Rail Depot, which had a 1,500-seat auditorium on the top floor. The concert, which was oversold, turned into a disaster as countless angry fans found themselves left outside the auditorium. As windows were smashed and rioting ensued, Jenny Lind was reported (probably falsely by Barnum's publicity machine) to have climbed up one of the building's two stone towers and sung to appease the mob below.

In 1927, when the station was being torn down, the railroad lawyer Henry M. Aldrich had the tower dismantled and transported to land he owned in North Truro. The brick-by-brick reconstruction of the tower took more than two months and involved the labor of five men. Why Aldrich was motivated to go to such trouble is not

TUNEFUL TOWER

WHAT: Jenny Lind Tower

WHERE: Off S Highland Rd. in North Truro

COST: Free

PRO TIP: Another intriguing structure to climb is Scargo Tower atop Scargo Hill in Dennis. A memorial for the Tobey family, the stone tower affords views on the bay side of Cape Cod from Provincetown to the Sagamore Bridge.

The Jenny Lind Tower is a reminder of what can happen when a concert is oversold.

known, although it is believed to stem from his family's association with the railroad. The only documented use of the tower is when Aldrich and his family watched the total solar eclipse of August 1932 from the top.

Aldrich descendants donated the tower to the Cape Cod National Seashore in 1961. While there is no road to the tower, which is located roughly between the Highland Lighthouse and the decommissioned North Truro Air Force Station, hikers can make their way to it on a narrow path through the scrubby vegetation. Inside the tower are stairs and ramps leading to the top for panoramic views over the dunes and woodlands.

According to local lore, Jenny Lind's ghost sings from the tower on nights when the ghost of Goody Hallett, the so-called Witch of Wellfleet, screams and curses at passing ships. Lind's sweet singing is believed to drive away Hallett or perhaps calm her rage.

DAYS ON THE BEACH

What's the story behind the row of 22 identical vintage cottages in North Truro?

You can't miss these iconic white cottages with sea-foam-green shutters lining the bay on your drive to Provincetown. Even if you haven't driven by, you've likely seen them in photos, paintings, or TV commercials. These retro cottages have appeared everywhere from a *Vogue* fashion shoot to a Camaro commercial to *The Price Is Right* TV show.

The 420-square-foot bungalows, set 18 feet apart on a private beach, took shape in 1931 after Joseph and Amelia Days scrapped a plan to move their own house to this strip of sand on Cape Cod Bay. After taking their Provincetown house apart and hauling it to the Truro beachfront—locals called it "Days' Folly"—they gave up and torched the fractured house in a giant beach bonfire.

Joe, who owned a construction company, then devised a new plan to build two-bedroom vacation cottages at the site. Amelia gave each a plaque with a flower name.

The cottages have found fame in paintings by John Dowd and photographs by Joel Meyerowitz.

Across the street, Joe's crew built Days Market—which is still open—and even converted a gas station into a 23rd cottage. Families began renting summer after summer, forging lifelong friendships with their cottage neighbors.

The Days family sold the colony in 2017, and the cabins are now condos. Many are vacation rentals, and some owners have added amenities such as smart TVs to the no-frills bungalows. But for those who retreat to this summer getaway, it's all about simplicity: the salt air, the views, falling asleep to the sound of the waves. As one guest of Daisy Cottage put it: "You wake up and you're right on the beach. Coffee, waves, beach, sand. There really isn't anything better."

DAYS COTTAGES

WHAT: Iconic row of vintage beach cottages

WHERE: 276 Shore Rd., North Truro

COST: Vacation rentals vary by season.

PRO TIP: Pick up Days Cottages merchandise, such as coffee mugs, at dayscottages.com. Proceeds will fund a new seawall for the colony. Contact dayscottages. rentals for information on renting Daisy Cottage.

The cottages are a 10-minute drive or a four-mile bike ride from Provincetown.
Photo by Massachusetts Office of Travel & Tourism

SANDY CASTLES

What is the story behind the dune shacks and their allure for so many artists?

They may be some of the humblest dwellings to be found on Cape Cod, but few draw as much fascination as the 19 dilapidated shacks, all lacking running water, electricity, and road access, scattered among the massive sand dunes not far beyond the streets of Provincetown. From the 1920s onward, the enclave of shacks, now part of the Peaked Hill Bars Historic District within the Cape Cod National Seashore, has been a creative gathering place for the likes of Eugene O'Neill, Tennessee Williams, Jack Kerouac, Jackson Pollock, Willem de Kooning, Annie Dillard, and many others.

The shacks are surrounded by hills of loose and shifting sand, some as high as 100 feet, so getting anywhere near them requires either a strenuous hike or taking a van tour like the one we booked with Art's Dune Tours. After we boarded the heavy-duty van equipped with special tires to handle the rugged terrain, owner Rob Costa explained that his dad, Art, who founded the company in 1946, was from a family of immigrant Portuguese fishermen and wanted a different career path when he returned home from World War II.

Entering the dune area, Rob pointed out the lush vegetation spilling over the dunes, a tangle of bayberry bushes, choke cherries, and rosa rugosa, wild roses native to the Orient that are often dried to make rose hips. "There are also wild beach plums here, which make good jam and jelly," Rob said. "I like to use them to make vodka."

ART'S DUNE TOURS

WHAT: A company providing van tours of the Peaked Hill Bars Historic District

WHERE: 4 Standish St., Provincetown

COST: $40 for the one-hour Daily Dunes tour

PRO TIP: In addition to Daily Dunes, Art's Dune Tours offers extended Sunset Tours with time to spend at a beach and watch the sun setting over the ocean. Some also include a dinner served on the sand.

Left: *Author Annie Dillard is among those who sought privacy in this dune shack. Photo by Maria Lenhart.* Right: *Rob Costa of Art's Dune Tours. Photo by Linda Humphrey*

As we took our roller-coaster ride up and down the dunes, Rob related a story of when the dunes were used as a setting for the original 1968 *Thomas Crown Affair* movie with Steve McQueen and Faye Dunaway. "My mom had a huge crush on Steve McQueen and was insistent on baking him one of her delicious coffee cakes," he said.

Soon we spied a humble shack that was once inhabited by author Annie Dillard, whose books include the Pulitzer Prize–winning *Pilgrim at Tinker Creek* and *The Maytrees*, a novel set in Provincetown. Rob explained that dune shacks were originally built by "surf men" responsible for scouting out shipwrecks, a frequent occurrence in the 19th and early 20th centuries before the Cape Cod Canal opened. Creative people drawn to the burgeoning Provincetown arts scene took over some of the shacks and also built new ones.

Today, only one of the 19 remaining shacks is privately owned. The rest have been acquired by the National Park Service, which leases some of them to artists and writers under a residency program. Currently there are legal battles going on between the park service and long-time shack dwellers over who has the right to occupy them.

Leasing a dune shack doesn't include the right to drive a vehicle to reach it. Those who need a ride must call a dunes tour operator for a lift.

143

PORTUGAL ON THE CAPE

What are ways to enjoy a taste of Portuguese culture on the Cape?

With the Azores island group and mainland Portugal exactly due east of the sandy fist of Cape Cod, it's little wonder that Portuguese heritage is easily found in Provincetown and other places on the Cape. When the whaling industry began booming in the 1840s, Portuguese and Azorean fishermen flocked to southeastern Massachusetts, establishing communities in places such as Provincetown and Falmouth. Their legacy lives on with festivities, art installations, and delicious items found in bakeries and seafood restaurants.

Among Provincetown's most arresting features are the outsized black-and-white portraits of Portuguese matriarchs gazing out from the side of a building on the end of Fisherman's Wharf. Called *They Also Face the Sea*, the iconic images were installed by artist Ewa Nogiec and photographer Norma Holt in 2003 as a tribute to the women of the Portuguese fishing community.

The murals of Portuguese matriarchs are part of Provincetown's rich Portuguese heritage. Photo courtesy of Massachusetts Office of Travel & Tourism

The Provincetown Portuguese Festival, an annual event held over four days in late June, celebrates the town's seafaring heritage with music, dancing, parades, foods, games, and more. It's capped off by the Blessing of the Fleet, with decorated boats parading through the town to receive a bishop's blessing for a safe and prosperous year on the water.

Chances to enjoy Portuguese goods are available throughout the year at places like the Provincetown Portuguese Bakery, a popular spot to enjoy coffee and a truta, a crescent-shaped fried pastry filled with sweet potato laced with cinnamon and bourbon, or a malassada, a donut-like confection dusted with sugar and sometimes filled with cream or jam. At the Lobster Pot, a Provincetown landmark where a neon sign of the red crustacean has delighted passersby for generations, specialties like Portuguese kale soup and seafood stews flavored with linguica are menu highlights.

One reason that Provincetown has long been a safe haven for the LGBTQ+ community is that Portuguese immigrants were welcoming to gay lodgers as far back as the Great Depression. While the wives of Portuguese fishermen were wary of renting rooms to straight men while their husbands were away at sea, they felt safer around those they referred to as "nice boys."

DRAMATISTS IN THE DUNES

What role did Provincetown play in launching the careers of Tennessee Williams, Eugene O'Neill, and Marlon Brando?

While the Mississippi Delta is the place most often associated with Tennessee Williams, as is Connecticut with Eugene O'Neill, it's actually Provincetown where the two great playwrights found their footing.

O'Neill, who had already worked as a gold prospector in Honduras and as a seaman on a tramp steamer, was 28 years old in 1916 when he and other young artists vacationing in Provincetown formed the Provincetown Players. They turned a fishing shack on Captain Jack's Wharf into the Playwrights' Theater, the venue in which they performed their own plays, including O'Neill's *Bound East for Cardiff*. After receiving good reviews, the group soon moved on to New York's Greenwich Village but still called themselves the Provincetown Players.

Eventually penning such classics as *The Iceman Cometh* and *Long Day's Journey into Night*, O'Neill went on to win four Pulitzer Prizes and the Nobel Prize for Literature. One of his plays, *Ile*, was inspired by a Provincetown legend about a woman named Viola Cook said to have gone insane during a voyage to the Arctic.

As for Williams, he spent four summers in Provincetown in the 1940s. During those summers he worked on some of his best-known plays, including *The Glass Menagerie*, *A Streetcar*

Left: *Captain Jack's Wharf is a former stomping ground of Tennessee Williams and Eugene O'Neill.* Right: *Tennessee Williams in Provincetown, 1940s*

Named Desire, Summer and Smoke, Night of the Iguana, and *Suddenly Last Summer*. Again, Captain Jack's Wharf played a featured role, with Williams staying in a shack there and writing *The Glass Menagerie* on a borrowed typewriter with the sounds of waves lapping below. The playwright also found love and acceptance among the local artistic gay community and met his life partner, Frank Merlo, a working-class Italian American from New Jersey.

Today, Williams's prolific output—he wrote at least 90 dramatic works—are the focus of the annual Provincetown Tennessee Williams Theater Festival that takes place over a three-day weekend in September at various venues around town. Along with enjoying the festival, visitors can explore the dramatic legacy at Atlantic House or A-House, a watering hole with connections to both O'Neill and Williams that is believed to be the country's oldest gay bar.

When Marlon Brando was being considered for his iconic role as Stanley in the Broadway production of *A Streetcar Named Desire* in the summer of 1947, director Elia Kazan sent him to Provincetown to audition for Tennessee Williams. Brando quickly squandered the bus fare Kazan gave him, so he had to hitchhike from New York to Provincetown. Not only was Williams thrilled with the handsome and talented young actor, he got him to do some plumbing work on his cabin.

PRIDE OVER PREJUDICE

How did Provincetown become an early LGBTQ+ safe haven?

Provincetown, the original landing spot of the *Mayflower* Pilgrims, has long been a place for seekers of freedom, especially for members of the LGBTQ+ community. The town's legacy as a rare, safe place to be openly gay stretches back for well over a century, intertwined with its development as a summer arts colony drawing painters, dramatists, novelists, and assorted freethinkers to its secluded beaches and cheap boarding houses operated by tolerant Portuguese families. Among the most celebrated of the gay artists drawn to Provincetown was Tennessee Williams, who spent four summers there in the 1940s and wrote *The Glass Menagerie* while staying at Captain Jack's Wharf in the West End.

By the 1950s, Provincetown was proudly embracing its thriving status as a gay resort with nightclubs featuring drag acts and cross-dressing waiters. A backlash ensued in 1952 when the town selectmen tried to shut the clubs down and called for an end to "the nests where the homosexuals congregate," but their attempt to stifle gay culture ultimately failed. More recently, Provincetown was the backdrop for scenes in the hit movie *Bros*, the first major studio film featuring an all LGBTQ+ cast (and much of the crew).

Clad in a mix of historically accurate and inaccurate (sequins and feathers) attire, Provincetown tour guide Brent Thomas portrays 17th-century historical figure Anne Hutchinson. The excursion, a mix of historic tour and stand-up comedy, delves into the cultural evolution of this one-of-a-kind resort town. Tickets for the tour are $30 and are available on TripAdvisor.

Top: *The Rainbow Flag flies free in Provincetown.* Inset: *View from the top of the Pilgrim Monument. Photos courtesy of Massachusetts Office of Travel & Tourism*

OUT AND ABOUT

WHAT: Pilgrim Monument and Provincetown Museum

WHERE: 1 High Pole Hill Rd., Provincetown

COST: $20.94 adults

PRO TIP: Don't miss the splashy beach bar and outdoor seating with bay views at the Canteen.

A new permanent exhibit at the Pilgrim Monument and Provincetown Museum, *An Anecdotal LGBTQ+ History of the Last Century of Provincetown*, tells a compelling story through artifacts, recorded interviews, and short documentaries curated by the Generations Project. Among them are the high heels and elaborate garments worn by the Hat Sisters, a gay couple whose onstage antics and fabulous headwear were a local entertainment staple for decades. Other parts of the exhibit chronicle the dark days of the AIDS epidemic when Provincetown became a sanctuary for patients whose own communities had shut them out.

In a recorded interview, the lesbian painter Ilona Rice Simpkin, who died at age 101 in 2021 and lived most of her life above her gallery on Commercial Street, says of Provincetown, "In the whole world, it's about the most open, caring, and kind town."

SCREEN GEMS, PART TWO

How did two iconic island theaters survive so many lives?

Few theaters in America have as long and peripatetic a history as the Dreamland in Nantucket. Originally built in 1829 as a Quaker meetinghouse, the building subsequently served as a straw-hat factory and a roller skating rink. Then, in 1883, it was moved to the Brant Point area and became part of the Nantucket Hotel. The structure was moved again in 1906, this time put on a barge and floated across Nantucket Harbor to its current location, where it opened as Smith and Blanchard's Moving Picture Show before being renamed Dreamland Theater in 2011. For nearly a century the Dreamland served as the island's premier entertainment venue, starting with vaudeville performances and eventually first-run movies.

After the building was sold in 2004, the Dreamland stood empty for several years as various redevelopment plans for the old theater fell through. In 2007, the Dreamland Foundation, a consortium of Nantucket summer residents led by Google CEO Eric Schmidt, purchased the building with the intent of operating a

SCREEN SURVIVORS

WHAT: The Dreamland Film, Theater & Cultural Center; The Strand Theatre

WHERE: 17 S Water St., Nantucket; 11 Oak Bluffs Ave., Oak Bluffs

COST: Ticket prices vary according to event.

PRO TIP: Starting at $50, annual memberships offered by the Dreamland include $5 off movie tickets, free admission to selected films and live theater performances, and free popcorn.

The Quaker meetinghouse that was the Dreamland Theater's original incarnation was the frequent scene of antislavery meetings during the pre–Civil War era.

performing arts/community center. Their plans were realized with the Dreamland Film, Theatre & Cultural Center, a new structure that incorporates the original beams from the 1829 meetinghouse into its design. It offers two theaters presenting films and live performances and spaces for community events.

On Martha's Vineyard, the Strand Theatre in Oak Bluffs has been through a few incarnations of its own. Originally built as an Oddfellows Hall, it was converted to a theater in 1915 by an Irish immigrant named Michael Keegan who believed strongly in the future of moving pictures. After changing hands in the 1930s, the theater received a makeover that is still in evidence today, including a stucco exterior, leather seats, and a bright color scheme in red, green, and silver.

The Strand remained in business until 2011, when it was shuttered and, like so many old movie houses, faced an uncertain future. For a few years, a bicycle rental business operated out of the lobby. It was eventually rescued by fundraising efforts from the nonprofit Martha's Vineyard Theater Foundation and reopened in 2015. However, the theater was again in jeopardy when it closed during the pandemic in 2020. Fortunately, there appears to be a Hollywood ending in the works. Leased in 2022 by Steve and Dorothy Capers, producers of the annual Martha's Vineyard Comedy Festival, the theater is once again showing movies as well as hosting fundraisers, talks, and special events.

The Dreamland Theater has been a Quaker meetinghouse, hat factory, and roller skating rink. Photo by Linda Humphrey

HEARTBREAK HOTEL

Is this old-world-Nantucket hotel also a haunted mansion?

The gleaming 19th-century rooms of Nantucket's Jared Coffin House hotel have hosted Melville, Thoreau, President Ulysses S. Grant, and the occasional ghost. Built in 1845 by whaling merchant Coffin, the brick mansion is a happening spot, its stylish guests dining under strings of lights on the patio.

With a history stretching over 175 years, the mansion is chock full of ghost stories. In 2010, a guest checking into Room 303 found a young woman in a Victorian gown sitting in the corner, smiling at him. Noting that she was transparent, he fled and promptly checked out. Six years later, another guest strolled into the lobby for an early breakfast and found just one other diner, a young woman sitting by the wall. As he walked over to speak to her, she vanished.

Coffin sold his mansion in 1847, when it opened as a public house—as hotels were then known—called the Ocean House. In the years before this faraway island became a vacation hot spot for the global elite, from 1945 to 1960, the Ocean House was known as *the* place to have affairs, said tour guide Bill Jamieson.

Some even checked into the Ocean House looking to meet someone on the wraparound porch. Legend has it that guests would get their keys and then mingle on the porch, where those who were seated were taken, and those who were standing were available, Jamieson said.

The notorious porch was demolished in the early 1960s as the Ocean House gave way to a restored Jared Coffin House. Acquired by White Elephant Resorts in 2004, the pre–Civil War landmark

---

The captain of the ill-fated whaling expedition that inspired Melville's *Moby-Dick*, George Pollard Jr., once lived in the red-shingled saltbox house across the street.

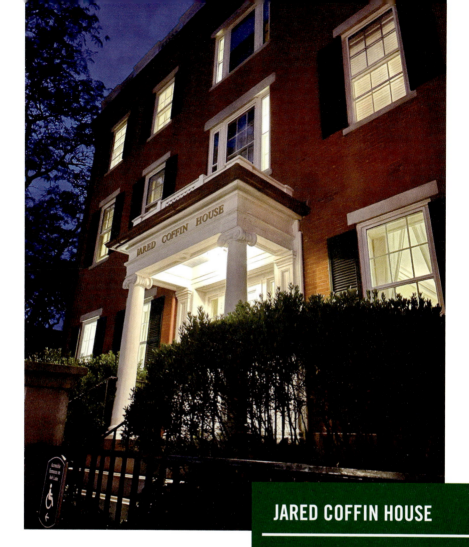

The hotel's historic Nantucket Tap Room restaurant was a billiard saloon and gentleman's smoking room back in the 1800s. Photo by Kristi Towey

was fully renovated in 2020, adding four new suites. You'll find complimentary coffee and pastries in the library each morning. . . . Keep your eyes peeled for vanishing guests.

JARED COFFIN HOUSE

WHAT: 19th-century mansion turned storied hotel

WHERE: 29 Broad St., Nantucket

COST: Varies by season

PRO TIP: For more information on Bill Jamieson's Nantucket Walking Tours and Notorious Nantucket Tour, contact whjamieson@gmail or call 774-325-8972.

NANTUCKET'S ASTRONOMICAL GENIUS

Where can you trace the legacy of astronomer Maria Mitchell?

Even before there was Marie Curie, Nantucket laid claim to a pioneering female scientist of its own. She was Maria Mitchell, an avid amateur astronomer who became the first American to discover a comet. Born to Quaker parents in 1818, Mitchell, under the guidance and encouragement of her schoolteacher father, William, developed an early passion for astronomy. As a young girl she assisted sailors in navigating the seas with her celestial calculations.

In 1847, with the use of a two-inch telescope, Mitchell spied an unknown comet from the rooftop of a bank on Main Street. The discovery catapulted her to worldwide fame, leading to a professorship at Vassar College and admittance to leading scientific organizations that previously had few or no female members. Mitchell traveled the world on the lecture circuit, even receiving a medal from the King of Denmark.

After Mitchell's death in 1889, her friends, family, and students formed the Maria Mitchell Association, dedicated to scientific education and preserving the places on Nantucket associated with her life. These include the

STAR POWER

WHAT: Maria Mitchell Association

WHERE: 4 Vestal St., Nantucket

COST: $22 adults, $12 children

PRO TIP: Guided tours of the Historic Mitchell House are available from mid-June through the end of August. The house also hosts programs focusing on the Mitchell family's daily life and their contributions to Nantucket history.

Historic Mitchell House, her gray-shingled childhood home filled with personal items such as beer mugs, opera glasses, and a Dolland telescope; and the adjacent Maria Mitchell Research Center, where a natural sciences collection, archives, and laboratory now occupy William Mitchell's former schoolhouse.

In addition, the association oversees the Loines Observatory, a venue for public astronomy programs and an active research observatory that includes antique telescopes and more than 8,000 glass photographic plates of the sky, recording observations made between 1913 and 1995. Still other holdings of the association include the Maria Mitchell Natural Science Museum, which features exhibits of live animals and hands-on activities for kids, and Maria Mitchell Aquarium, which offers Marine Ecology Walks where participants can observe the feeding habits of nocturnal sea creatures and assist in the collection, identification, and sorting of specimens.

Marine scientists associated with the Maria Mitchell Aquarium lead excursions during the winter to Muskeget Island, located just offshore from Nantucket, where the birthing of hundreds of gray seal pups can be witnessed.

The Historic Mitchell House displays items from Maria Mitchell's childhood.

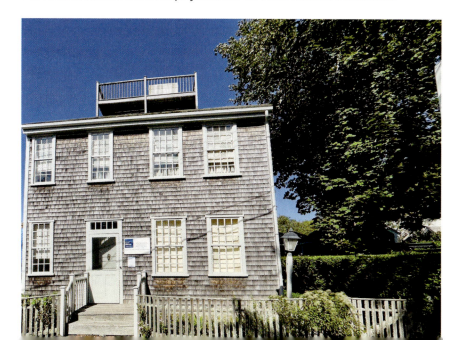

STARRY NIGHT

What's the story behind the Two Greeks, Nantucket's dazzling Greek Revival mansions?

The pair of Greek temple–like mansions taking shape on Main Street in the 1840s were the most extravagant homes the island had ever seen. As the last manors built by a whale-oil magnate, they were the scene of much revelry among Nantucket's elite, who danced under the stars in a ballroom with a circular oculus open to the sky.

Set among the island's simple Quaker houses and Georgian bricks, the colonnaded mansions were built for William Hadwen, who first arrived on Nantucket for the wedding of his cousin Nathaniel Barney to Eliza Starbuck. It was 1820, and the island's whaling heyday had hit a peak that would last throughout the 1830s.

Hadwen fell in love with the bride's older sister, Eunice Starbuck, and was soon seduced by the whaling industry as well. While Hadwen was a silversmith from Newport, Rhode Island, and Barney was a schoolteacher, they seized their chance to become whale-oil merchants, snapping up a house with a backyard whale-oil candle factory. By 1848, they owned a candle and oil refinery on Broad Street that is now the Whaling Museum.

A Greek Revival craze began to sweep the island in the rosy 1830s, beginning with classical elements such as doorways (note the porticoes of the Three Bricks, home to the three Starbuck brothers). Hadwen ushered in the temple-front facade in 1846, the same year that a fire destroyed some 250 buildings in town. His second mansion, added in 1847, is even more ornate than the

---

Summer interns staying at the Hadwen House have reported the sounds of glasses clinking together, laughter, and chairs being moved late at night, said tour guide Bill Jamieson.

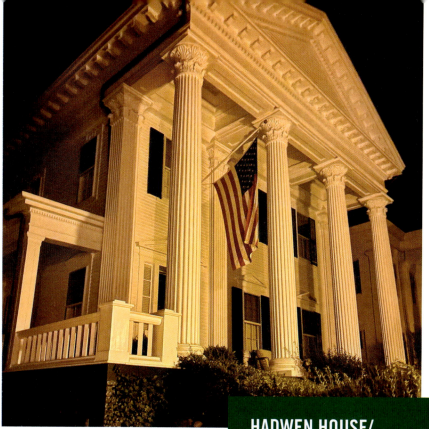

After the War of 1812, the island turned away from British architecture and embraced Greek Revival, which was all the rage during the whaling heyday of the 1830s to the Civil War. Above: 94 Main Street. Photo by Kristi Towey

HADWEN HOUSE/ THE TWO GREEKS

WHAT: Greek Revival mansion turned museum showcasing the opulence of the whaling era

WHERE: 96 Main St., Nantucket

COST: $10 adults, $5 ages 6–17

PRO TIP: Admission to the Whaling Museum includes entry to the Hadwen House.

first, with Corinthian columns, elaborate detailing, and the second-floor ballroom.

Now a house museum, Hadwen's home is one of few island residences of its age open to the public, offering a glimpse into the heady days of the whaling era. Alas, the mansion with the ballroom is now a private home.

WON'T YOU BE MY NANTUCKET NEIGHBOR?

Which TV legend is honored with a plaque in a historic church?

On Nantucket, you'll find an icon plaque at the century-old St. Paul's Church, over on the far wall. Surrounded by the words "Gentle, Kind + True," there's a picture of . . . is that Mister Rogers?

Indeed it is. Fred Rogers—the cardigan-wearing creator of the longest-running public television program in history, *Mister Rogers' Neighborhood*—was a much-loved summer fixture on the island and a member of St. Paul's.

MISTER ROGERS ICON PLAQUE

WHAT: A plaque honoring Mister Rogers near his church pew

WHERE: St. Paul's Episcopal Church, 20 Fair St., Nantucket

COST: Free

PRO TIP: A Fred Rogers Park is in the works on Easy Street, complete with a statue of Rogers in his red cardigan.

"Mister Rogers' neighborhood" on Nantucket was Smith's Point—known as Smith's—a spit of land at the far western end of Madaket known for brilliant sunsets. Fred and his wife, Joanne, found the title to their house in the toe of their Christmas stocking in the 1960s, a surprise gift from Fred's parents.

The couple had rented the rambling cottage—known as the Crooked House for its slight lean—in the summer of 1960, flying up from their Pittsburgh-area home with their year-old son, James. A second son, John, arrived a year later.

When the Crooked House needed a new foundation in 1980, Rogers asked the contractors to keep the cottage crooked.

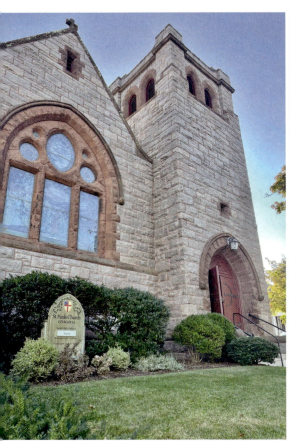

Fred and Joanne Rogers attended St. Paul's Episcopal Church on Nantucket. For a time, a red cardigan was draped over their pew, which is next to the wall plaque. Photos by Linda Humphrey

Rogers swam in Madaket Bay every day for exactly 17 minutes, asking a neighbor to blow into a conch shell when the time was up. To toast the end of summer, Fred and Chef Brockett, a character on the show, would host a breakfast for their Smith's Point neighbors at a beach or restaurant, the date kept secret until the night before. Brockett was an actor and not an actual chef, but no matter—it was all about being neighbors.

STARBUCKS, NOT THE COFFEE

What's the story behind the trio of identical brick mansions on Nantucket's Main Street?

If you can ignore the shiny Jeeps bumping over the cobblestones, Nantucket's Main Street appears much as it did in its whaling-era heyday.

The three matching brick manors at numbers 93, 95, and 97, with their striking row of classical porticos and Ionic columns, were built in 1838 by Joseph Starbuck, the wealthiest whale-oil merchant of his time. Fearing that his three sons would go off to sea, Starbuck offered to give each a mansion if they would stay on the island and work for the family business.

While posh mansions were springing up on Orange and Fair Streets at the time, Main Street—with its shoe-deep sand and candle-factory fumes—was just beginning to gentrify, its signature cobblestones added in 1837. (For a glimpse of 18th-century Main Street, check out the 1762 "typical Nantucket house" at number 84.)

Joseph Starbuck's daughters, meanwhile, did not get mansions, as they were expected to marry well. Eunice met her husband, William Hadwen, at her sister Eliza's wedding to Nathaniel Barney, and the two couples shared an estate at number 100 until Hadwen built the two opulent Greek Revival mansions, known as the Two

---

Is this family connected to the coffee company? Sort of. Starbucks was named for the Starbuck character in *Moby-Dick*, Herman Melville's 1851 novel. Melville drew inspiration for the book by researching Nantucket's prominent whaling families, where he found the Starbuck name.

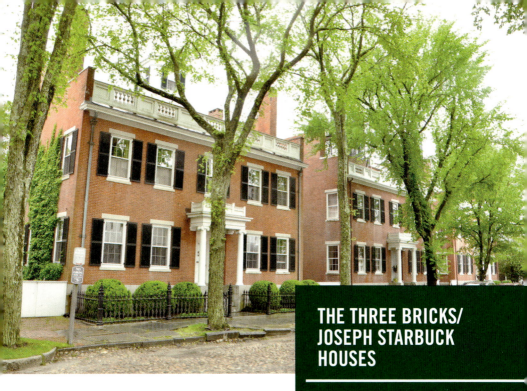

Brick houses were rare at the time, as few could afford to ship bricks to the island. Photo by William DeSousa-Mauk

Greeks, across the street from the Three Bricks in the 1840s.

By 1850, as the Starbuck compound bustled with 17 first cousins, once-forsaken Main Street had become the most sought-after address in town.

THE THREE BRICKS/ JOSEPH STARBUCK HOUSES

WHAT: Three identical 19th-century houses built for three brothers

WHERE: 93, 95, and 97 Main St., Nantucket

COST: Free to view from the street. $15 NPT Main Street walking tour.

PRO TIP: The Nantucket Preservation Trust (NPT) offers weekly architectural walking tours of Main Street from June to early October. Sign up at nantucketpreservation.org.

Grab coffee for the walk at local favorite Handlebar Cafe. (You won't find a Starbucks, as the island bans large chains.)

ISLAND ELIXIR

Where can you walk along the front yards of private, oceanview homes?

Often compared to the Cotswolds in England or a fairy tale, this Nantucket seaside village is known for its tiny, rose-covered cottages. Sconset (short for Siasconset) was a 17th-century fishing outpost, its adorable Snow White–style bungalows fashioned from antique fish shacks. The core of the oldest cottage, Auld Lang Syne at 6 Broadway, dates to about 1675.

Set on a bluff above the Atlantic, Sconset was an elixir to Nantucketers in the 1800s seeking to escape the whale-oil-refinery fumes in town. Fishermen expanded their gray-shingled one-room shacks with haphazard additions called warts, and in the late 1880s, developer Edward Underhill copied their enchanting design, including warts, T-shaped plans, and half-gable roofs.

Glamorous Broadway stars soon arrived on the new railroad, turning Underhill's cottages and this remote beach town into an actors' colony. With New York City theaters shuttered for the sweltering summer months, these big-name actors and writers bankrolled a theater and tennis club in 1899, the Sconset Casino. A "hall of amusement" never used for gambling, the casino is now primarily a private tennis club.

After wandering the narrow lanes of Broadway, Center, and Shell Streets, stroll along the Bluff Walk, a footpath overlooking the sea. As the dollhouse-sized cottages give way to opulent, oceanfront summer

SCONSET BLUFF WALK

WHAT: Ocean-view walk along the front yards of private homes

WHERE: Path begins near 21 Front St.

COST: $15 NPT walking tour. Bluff Walk is free.

PRO TIP: The Nantucket Preservation Trust (NPT) offers weekly guided architectural walking tours of Sconset from June to early October. Sign up at nantucketpreservation.org.

Top: *Sconset's roses are at their peak in late June and early July. Photos by Linda Humphrey.* Bottom: *Sconset's Bluff Walk. Photo by Kristi Towey*

homes and the sound of crashing waves, you'll walk along the edges of their lime-green front lawns, thanks to William Flagg, a late 1800s developer who required a public right of way in the deeds to his home lots.

Return to the early 1900s for lunch or dinner at the rose-covered Chanticleer, first opened as a tearoom by stage actress Agnes Everett.

The railroad was torn up in 1918, its tracks shipped off to Europe for the Allied war effort. Its passenger car is now the bar of the Club Car restaurant at One Main Street, in town.

A MIDSUMMER NIGHT'S DREAM

How did an 18th-century livestock barn become a summer house and eclectic museum?

Decades before the resort crowd arrived, two Philadelphia heiresses followed a herd of cows up the cobblestones of Nantucket's Main Street. It was the summer of 1929, and sisters Hanna and Gertrude Monaghan had arrived for the island's thriving art-colony scene, which began in the 1920s as whaling-era shacks, shanties, and boathouses were reimagined into art studios.

Gertrude, an artist, and Hanna, a writer and actress, were Quakers who saw art as an expression of their faith. When the cows led them to a 140-year-old barn tucked behind rows of sea captains' mansions, they envisioned Greater Light, their whimsical summer home and studio. They bought the dilapidated barn and began to transform it with architectural salvage and exotic furnishings picked up on their world travels, even during the Great Depression. Scavenging junkyards, demolished buildings, auction houses, and thrift stores, they designed every inch of the house themselves.

Months before finding the barn, Hanna had salvaged 12-foot-high wrought iron gates from a Pennsylvania junkyard. Shipped to Nantucket, they fit the door of the patio—once the pigsty—as if they had been custom-made. She spied the iron balconies at a Philadelphia demolition site, jumping out of a taxi to hand a bunch of cash to the foreman.

Stained-glass windows made of yellow wine bottles salvaged from a Philadelphia pub adorn Hanna's bedroom, while four cast-

Frank Swift Chase, a painter and teacher known as "the dean of Nantucket artists," led art classes on the island nearly every summer from 1920 to 1955.

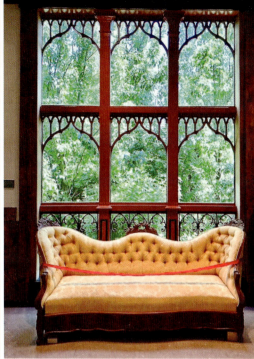

Top: *Hanna's bed was reimagined from the barn's horse trough. Note the wine-bottle windows, salvaged from a Philadelphia pub.* Bottom left and right: *Greater Light is a reference to Genesis 1:16: "God made two great lights—the greater light to govern the day and the lesser light to govern the night. He made the stars also." Photos courtesy of Massachusetts Office of Travel & Tourism*

GREATER LIGHT

WHAT: 18th-century livestock barn transformed into an art studio and summer oasis, now a museum

WHERE: 8 Howard St., Nantucket

COST: Free to visit

PRO TIP: For a full list of the classes and workshops taught at Greater Light, see nha.org/whats-on/programs/decorative-arts

off church windows—melded together in red painted frames to create French doors—open to the garden balcony, once the hayloft. The great-room window is crafted from another nine church windows.

Now owned by the Nantucket Historical Association, Greater Light is open for tours, art classes, and events, a tribute to the island's tradition of decorative arts and crafts.

A BASKET CASE

How is the Nantucket lightship basket interwoven with the island's history?

I was made on Nantucket. I'm strong and I'm stout. Don't lose me or burn me and I'll never wear out.

What kind of basket inspired early 20th-century craftsman Mitchell Ray to compose the above ditty? What kind of basket has commanded prices rivaling those of precious jewelry? What kind of basket has origins bound up in the days of whalers and lonely lightships? And, most important, what kind of basket is unique to a quaint and scrubby little island off the coast of southern Massachusetts?

It's the highly prized Nantucket lightship basket.

The original lightship baskets were made on board the *South Shoal Lightship*, a vessel moored off the rocky Nantucket coast during the 19th century to warn ships away from the treacherous shoals. Sailors, faced with dreary six-month assignments aboard the ship with nothing to do but clean the lamps and keep watch, passed the time by weaving their special sort of baskets.

Unlike the free-form baskets that characterize those from most other cultures, lightship baskets are woven around molds, a practice that gives the weave extraordinary consistency and precision. Because their staves and bottoms are cut and carved from wood, usually hickory or oak, they are possibly the sturdiest baskets ever developed. Originally designed as open baskets, more modern versions, sometimes called "friendship baskets," are fashioned into round or oval-shaped purses with handles and lids. Embellishments on top of the lids determine the price, which can range anywhere

---

Authentic Nantucket lightship baskets, which can take over 40 hours to make, have never been cheap. They sold for $2.50 back in the 1880s, the equivalent of a man's weekly wage.

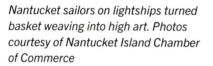
Nantucket sailors on lightships turned basket weaving into high art. Photos courtesy of Nantucket Island Chamber of Commerce

from $500 on up to hundreds of thousands for rare examples adorned with elaborate scrimshaw.

Island artisans still carry on the lightship basket tradition, among them Michael Kane who, after learning the craft from his grandparents, sold his first example in 1969 at Bette's Luncheonette in the Nantucket Pharmacy, owned by his mother. Today he has his own shop and online business. Prime examples of lightship baskets, both antique and contemporary, are often on exhibit at the Nantucket Historical Association's Whaling Museum and Hadwen House.

FALL FRIGHT

Who haunts Nantucket's Unitarian Meeting House?

A ghost walk through historic Nantucket town can feel especially spooky in autumn, when most of the historic houses have been shuttered for the season.

"You feel like you're in one of those last-person-left-on-Earth movies," said Bill Jamieson, who leads ghost tours through the island's lanterned, cobblestoned streets. Winding through dark and deserted lanes, our late-September tour with Jamieson led us to the 1809 Unitarian Meeting House, an island landmark with its iconic clock tower and gold dome. Also known as South Church, it's rumored to be haunted by its first minister, Reverend Seth Swift.

Stories of eerie activity here include a light flickering on the third floor, a radio turning off by itself (until the station was changed to classical) and the haunting sound of a pencil dropping, over and over, onto the floor.

It's said that Reverend Swift's ghost keeps watch over the sanctuary, scaring off mischievous

NANTUCKET GHOST WALK

WHAT: Ghost tour of historic Nantucket town. Contact whjamieson@gmail.com for more information.

WHERE: Meet at the Pacific National Bank, 61 Main St.

COST: $25 adults, $20 seniors

PRO TIP: The Unitarian Meeting House offers tours in July and August. Note the portrait of Reverend Seth Swift in Hendrix Hall.

With more than 800 buildings that predate the Civil War, Nantucket has no shortage of haunted sites. Among the others are the Nantucket Hotel & Resort, the Wauwinet, and the Chicken Box.

168

The Unitarian Meeting House, with its iconic clock tower and gold dome, is a landmark and beacon visible from five miles at sea. Photo courtesy of Massachusetts Office of Travel & Tourism

children. In the 1970s, as the story goes, church custodian Francis Morgan was working in the empty church when two local boys tapped on the vestry window. He let them inside to play, and they ran around upstairs in the sanctuary but somehow ended up back outside, tapping at the window again.

"The man upstairs chased us out," they said, "the man with the mean-looking eyes."

A few months later, Morgan's grandson grew uneasy as he explored the sanctuary. "I don't like that man," the boy said, pointing to the pulpit. "I don't like the way he's looking at me." Morgan saw no one. "That man there," the boy said, "the one with the nasty eyes."

Landfall Restaurant in Woods Hole.
Photo by Linda Humphrey

SOURCES

Shark! Site visits, https://archive.curbed.com/maps/the-ultimate-jaws-filming-location-map-of-marthas-vineyard, https://www.hgtv.com/lifestyle/real-estate/10-iconic-locations-from-jaws-and-what-they-look-like-today-pictures, https://ew.com/movies/jaws-filming-locations

Where I Like Being Me: Site visit to Abel's Hill Cemetery, Chilmark, https://www.mvtimes.com/2013/07/02/comic-john-belushis-good-man-bad-boy-persona-revealed-16206, https://www.chicagotribune.com/news/ct-xpm-2005-12-31-0512310150-story.html

Sound of Summer: Interview with Max Pinson, site visits to performances in Falmouth and at Cotuit Center for the Arts

Star Sanctuary (One and Two): Martha's Vineyard tour with Oak Bluffs Land and Wharf Co., https://galavante.com/destinations/celebrity-travel/celebs-on-marthas-vineyard, https://www.businessinsider.com/marthas-vineyard-obama-ceos-millionaires-celebs-homes-vacations-2019-12, https://www.hollywoodreporter.com/news/general-news/why-hollywood-hides-at-marthas-220053

Campy Site: Site visit and interview with Gingerbread Cottage Museum docent Nancy Block, Oak Bluffs: *The Cottage City Years on Martha's Vineyard* by Peter A. Jones (Arcadia Publications), https://www.mvcma.org

Vineyard Vanes: Site visit and tour, https://www.tuckandholand.com, https://newengland.com/today/high-art-with-weathervane-artist-anthony-holand-open-studio

Alley's General Storybook: site visit, https://www.onlyinyourstate.com/massachusetts/trading-post-ma

Down by the Sea: Site visits to Bass Hole Boardwalk and Menemsha, interview with William DeSousa-Mauk, tour and interview with Troy Neuenburg, Oak Bluffs Land & Wharf Co. Tours

Renaissance Woman: Site visits to Martha's Vineyard Museum's Dorothy West exhibit and to African American Heritage Trail of Martha's Vineyard, https://www.literaryladiesguide.com/author-biography/west-dorothy

Trail Blazers: Site visit to African American Heritage Trail of Martha's Vineyard, https://mvafricanamericanheritagetrail.org, https://vineyardgazette.com/news/2023/05/24/trail-25-years

Canal Zone: Site visit to Cape Cod Canal Visitors Center, canal cruise with Hy-Line Cruises, https://hylinecruises.com/cape-cod-canal-cruises

Pilgrims' Convenience Store: Site visit and interview with docent Jeremy Davis, https://www.capecodtimes.com/story/news/2021/06/21/aptucxet-trading-post-bourne-not-on-original-site-history-buff-says/5294680001

White House to Gray Gables: Site visit, interview with Tom Lyons, treasurer of the Bourne Historical Society

Heart of Glass: Site visits to Sandwich Glass Museum and Glass Town Cultural District. https://sandwichglassmuseum.org

Crowded House: Site visit and interview with historical archaeologist David Wheelock, https://www.wingfamily.org

Sweet Spot by Smiling Pool: Site visit and interview with Jam Kitchen owner Emalee Pierce, https://thorntonburgess.org/green-briar-nature-center

Abbey Road: Site visit and interview with Belfry Inn owner Christopher Wilson, https://www.belfryinn.com

Sentimental Journey: Site visit and ride on the Cape Cod Central Railroad Dinner Train excursion, https://www.capetrain.com

Coffee to Give a Hoot About: Site visits, https://www.socoffee.co

Gearhead Garage: Site visits to Heritage Museums & Gardens, Toad Hall Classic Car Museum, https://capecodclassics.org

Spirits in the Stacks: Site visit and interview with owner James Visbeck, https://www.isaiahthomasbooks.com, *Haunted Cape Cod & the Islands* by Mark Jasper (On Cape Cod Publications)

People of the First Light: Site visit, https://mashpeewampanoagtribe-nsn.gov

Dylan's Strangest Gig: Site visit to Sea Crest Beach Hotel, https://www.independent.co.uk/arts-entertainment/music/features/on-the-road-with-dylan-485340.html, https://www.newyorker.com/culture/cultural-comment/the-chaotic-magic-of-bob-dylans-rolling-thunder-revue

Saltwater Park: Site visits, interview with Lucy Helfrich, Director of Program Services for Falmouth's 300 Committee Land Trust

New England's Southern Charm: site visit, interview with innkeeper Pattie Laubhan, Falmouth's Museums on the Green Tour with Debbie Neal, Museums on the Green archives: "Falmouth in 1850" by W.H. Hewins, Falmouth's Town Clerk. Dated Oct. 2, 1924, interview with Meg Costello, research manager, Falmouth Historical Society/Museums on the Green, *A History through Houses: Cape Cod's Varied Residential Architecture* by Jaci Conry (Down East Books)

Broadway by the Sea: Site visits and interview with Executive and Artistic Director Mark A. Pearson, interviews with 2019 cast members Laura Lydia Paruzynski, Mitchell McVeigh, Andrey Vdovenko, Rachel Querreveld, Ryan Wolpert, and Gabby Gonzalez.

The High Life: Site visits, tour and interview with docent Jennifer Walker, highfieldhallandgardens.org

Caribbean on the Cape: Site visit and participation in Jamaica Night, https://www.coonamessettfarm.com, https://www.nytimes.com/2022/07/06/travel/cape-cod-jamaican-food.html

On the Lookout: Site visits to the Knob, site visit to Woods Hole Oceanographic Institute's Ocean Science Discovery Center, savebuzzardsbay.org

How the Cows Came Home: Site visits, https://www.capecodtimes.com/picture-gallery/news/2021/10/26/cape-cod-ma-woods-strange-locations-bog-house-cattle-tunnel-boundary-marker-cahoon-canal/8451083002

Tale of Two Capes: Site visits, https://www.capecodcvmuseum.org, http://www.zuhmi.org

Café with a Conscience: Site visit, https://www.brcapecod.com

Play Ball!: https://www.capecodbaseball.org, https://ydredsox.com/its-back-yd-red-sox-bring-back-famous-donut-burgers-in-2023

Ice Cream in Camelot: Site visit, https://www.fourseasicecream.com

The Very Witching Time of Night: Ghost Hunters Tour of Barnstable Village with Derek Bartlett

Vonnegut's Saab Story: https://www.vonnegutlibrary.org/wp-content/uploads/2009/12/MSADA-AUGUST-Vonnegut-single-pages.pdf, https://inthesetimes.com/article/have-i-got-a-car-for-you

Catch a Show—or a Ghost: Site visit, *A History of Theater on Cape Cod* by Sue Mellen (History Press), https://www.wickedlocal.com/story/bourne-courier/2006/04/13/vonnegut-was-among-friends-at/40380175007

A Storied Past: Site visit and interview with library director Lucy Loomis, https://www.sturgislibrary.org

Colonial Graffiti: Site visit, Ghost Hunters Tour with Derek Bartlett

The Pirate, the Witch, and the *Whydah*: site visit, discoverpirates.com

Cruising the Old King's Highway: Site drive, site visit to Hallet's Store, interview with owner Charlie Clark, https://youtu.be/19eC9f7YNpk; Katie Clancy & Sarah Lapsley Martin featuring architect Mary Ann Agresti and produced by *Cape Cod & the Islands* magazine

Somewhere, Beyond the Sea, Part Two: site visits to Dyer Pond and to Wellfleet Chamber of Commerce information Booth, https://www.boston.com/travel/travel/2022/06/21/mass-has-one-of-the-best-secret-beaches-in-the-u-s-according-to-southern-living, https://www.forbes.com/sites/bethgreenfield/2012/08/15/wellfleet-ponds-are-secret-cape-cod-treasures/?sh=2d1958ab2ad4, https://www.cbsnews.com/boston/news/old-ladies-against-underwater-garbage-cape-cod-ponds

Summer Playdates: Site visits, *A History of Theater on Cape Cod* by Sue Mellen (History Press), https://www.capeplayhouse.com/about-us, https://www.melodytent.org

A Little Night Music: *Cape Encounters* by Dan Gordon and Gary Joseph (Cockle Cove Press); *Haunted Cape Cod & the Islands* by Mark Jasper (On Cape Publications), *Haunted Yarmouth: Ghosts and Legends from the Cape* by Paul Cote and the Historical Society of Old Yarmouth (Haunted America Press), chapterhousecapecod.com

Gorey's Haunt: Site visit, interview with Gregory Hischak, director of the Edward Gorey House. edwardgoreyhouse.org

On Location: site visit, https://parnassusbooks.com

The Uninvited: Site visit, *Haunted Cape Cod* by Barbara Sillery (Haunted America Press), oldyarmouthinn.com

Who Stole the Portrait of Captain Hallet?: Site visit and tour, https://www.wickedlocal.com/story/register/2015/07/24/portrait-mystery/33810667007

Broadway to Bog: Site visit, http://anniescrannies.com

Sold!: Site visit, https://www.eldreds.com, https://www.capecodtimes.com/story/news/2021/10/23/eldred-women-auction-fight-gender-disparity-art-world-sale-representation-contemporary-19-20-century/8519466002, https://www.antiquesandthearts.com/women-artists-take-a-star-turn-at-eldreds

Into the Woods: site visit and meeting with Tina Holl, https://www.bostonglobe.com/metro/2014/10/07/harry-holl-created-pottery-and-art-scargo-pottery-dennis

Brewster's Wonderland: site visit, Crosbymansion.com, *A History through Houses: Cape Cod's Varied Residential Architecture* by Jaci Conry (Down East Books), interviews with Richard Archer, Crosby Mansion Properties Manager, and docents Deborah Jacobs, Mary Ann Starr, and Dede O'Neil

Farm to Tables: Site visit and tour with Assistant Farm Manager Kevin Nadeau, chatham-barsinn.com

Lodging and Spirits: Site visit, *Ghost of the Orleans Inn: A Cape Cod Mystery* by Ed Maas (Paraclete Press); *Haunted Cape Cod & the Islands* by Mark Jasper (On Cape Publications).

This Rescue Inspired a Disney Movie: Site visit to Rock Harbor to tour the CG36500, site visit to Coast Guard Heritage Museum, Barnstable, https://time.com/4197131/the-finest-hours-true-story

Going Quackers: Site visit, https://ducksinthewindow.com

Escape Rooms: https://capecodxplore.com/cape-cod-inns-on-the-underground-railroad/, https://www.capecodtimes.com/story/news/2001/02/25/ties-to-freedom/51003491007

Training Days: Site visit to Chatham Railroad Museum and interview with docent Jeff Gordon, https://www.chathamrailroadmuseum.com

Sea Change: Seal cruise with Monomoy Island Excursions, Harwich, monomoysealcruise.com, https://capecodxplore.com/monomoy-island, https://www.nytimes.com/2013/08/17/us/thriving-in-cape-cods-waters-gray-seals-draw-fans-and-foes.

Screen Gems (One and Two): Site visits, https://capecinema.org, https://chathamorpheum.org, https://www.nantucketdreamland.org/shows/showing-today, https://strandtheatre-marthasvineyard.com

Twenty-Two Years at Sea: Site visit and interview with National Park Ranger Brent Ellis

Night Lights: Site visit bonfire with National Seashore rangers, *Explorer's Guide: Cape Cod, Martha's Vineyard & Nantucket* by Kim Grant and Katy Ward (The Countryman Press). https://www.nps.gov/caco/planyourvisit/permitsandreservations.htm

Far from the Madding Summer Crowds: site visit, https://ccmht.org/,https://www.boston.com/travel/travel/2022/06/21/mass-has-one-of-the-best-secret-beaches-in-the-u-s-according-to-southern-living

Outer Cape Pioneers: https://www.nytimes.com/2022/08/13/style/wellfleet.html, *A History through Houses: Cape Cod's Varied Residential Architecture* by Jaci Conry (History Press), https://youtu.be/Ev_pFc6NESA

Jam & Bread: Site visits to BriarLane Jams & Jellies, PB Boulangerie Bistro, Maison Villatte. https://www.travelandleisure.com/trip-ideas/the-best-of-cape-cod, https://www.foodandwine.com/travel/restaurants/best-bakeries-in-america, https://www.bostonglobe.com/lifestyle/travel/2016/07/19/continuing-jam-cape

Hopper's Light Fantastic: Site visit to Highland Lighthouse and Highland House Museum, https://www.nytimes.com/2008/08/10/travel/10cultured.html?smid=nytcore-ios-share&referringSource=articleSha; https://www.smithsonianmag.com/arts-culture/hopper-156346356

Ode to a Swedish Nightingale: Site visit, https://www.capecod.com/lifestyle/the-story-of-the-jenny-lind-tower, https://provincetownmagazine.com/index.php/2019/09/18/the-tower-of-truro

Days on the Beach: Site visit, https://www.bostonmagazine.com/property/2017/06/06/days-cottages-truro

Sandy Castles: Tour and interview with Rob Costa, owner of Art's Dune Tours, https://www.smithsonianmag.com/arts-culture/what-do-jackson-pollock-tennessee-williams-and-norman-mailer-have-in-common-89958513

Portugal on the Cape: Site visits, http://wanderlust-tours.com/portuguese-heritage-on-cape-cod/, https://ptowntourism.com/history-and-legacy, https://newenglandhistoricalsociety.com/how-portuguese-immigrants-came-to-new-england

Dramatists in the Dunes: Site visits, https://capecodwave.com/tennessee-williams-provincetown-memory-eternity, https://www.bbc.com/culture/article/20141006-brandos-breakthrough, *A History of Theater on Cape Cod* by Sue Mellen (History Press), https://www.twptown.org

Pride over Prejudice: Site visits, https://newenglandhistoricalsociety. com/how-ptown-got-so-gay-gay-gay, https://www.capecodtimes.com/ story/entertainment/2022/09/08/ provincetown-century-lgbtq-history-reveal-museum-exhibit-pilgrim-monument-tolerance-open-hat-sister/7854248001, https://www.capecodtimes.com/ story/entertainment/2022/09/08/ provincetown-century-lgbtq-history-reveal-museum-exhibit-pilgrim-monument-tolerance-open-hat-sister/7854248001

Heartbreak Hotel: Site visit, Notorious Nantucket Tour with Bill Jamieson, jaredcoffinhouse.com

Nantucket's Astronomical Genius: Site visits, https://www.mariamitchell. org, https://www.womenshistory.org/ education-resources/biographies/maria-mitchell

Starry Night: Site visit, interview with Malcolm MacNab, Hadwen House Museum Guide, Nantucket Preservation Trust walking tour of Main Street with Rita Carr, director of media and communications, *A Walk Down Main Street: the Houses and Their Histories* by Betsy Tyler, 2006 (A Nantucket Preservation Trust Publication).

Won't You Be My Nantucket Neighbor?: site visit to St. Paul's Church, https:// www.nytimes.com/2019/11/19/ magazine/mr-rogers.html, https:// newengland.com/yankee/history/mister-rogerss-nantucket, Interview with Shantaw Bloise-Murphy, Nantucket's director of culture and tourism

Starbucks, Not the Coffee: Site visit, Nantucket Preservation Trust walking tour with Rita Carr, director of media and communications, *A Walk Down Main Street: the Houses and Their Histories* by Betsy Tyler, 2006 (A Nantucket Preservation Trust Publication), https://www.mentalfloss. com/article/19385/does-starbucks-have-any-relation-starbuck-family

Island Elixir: Site visit, *A Walk Down Broadway: A Self-Guided Walking Tour Through Sconset's Historic Core* by Betsy Tyler (A Nantucket Preservation Trust Publication), https://www. siasconsetcivicassociation.org/History, nha.org

Basket Case: Site visits, https://nha.org, https://michaelkaneslightshipbaskets.com

Fall Fright: *Nantucket Ghosts* by Blue Balliett (Down East Books), Nantucket Ghost Walk with tour guide Bill Jamieson

Home in Sconset.
Photo courtesy of William DeSousa-Mauk

INDEX

Wellfleet Drive-In.
Photo courtesy of Massachusetts
Office of Travel & Tourism